T0291400

Advanced Introduction to Negotiation

Elgar Advanced Introductions are stimulating and thoughtful introductions to major fields in the social sciences, business and law, expertly written by the world's leading scholars. Designed to be accessible yet rigorous, they offer concise and lucid surveys of the substantive and policy issues associated with discrete subject areas.

The aims of the series are two-fold: to pinpoint essential principles of a particular field, and to offer insights that stimulate critical thinking. By distilling the vast and often technical corpus of information on the subject into a concise and meaningful form, the books serve as accessible introductions for undergraduate and graduate students coming to the subject for the first time. Importantly, they also develop well-informed, nuanced critiques of the field that will challenge and extend the understanding of advanced students, scholars and policy-makers.

For a full list of titles in the series please see the back of the book. Recent titles in the series include:

Sustainable Careers
Jeffrey H. Greenhaus and Gerard A. Callanan

Business and Human Rights
Peter T. Muchlinski

Spatial Statistics
Daniel A. Griffith and Bin Li

The Sociology of the Self
Shanyang Zhao

Artificial Intelligence in Healthcare
Tom Davenport, John Glaser and Elizabeth Gardner

Central Banks and Monetary Policy
Jakob de Haan and Christiaan Pattipeilohy

Megaprojects
Nathalie Drouin and Rodney Turner

Social Capital
Karen S. Cook

Elections and Voting
Ian McAllister

Negotiation
Leigh Thompson and Cynthia S. Wang

Advanced Introduction to

Negotiation

LEIGH THOMPSON

J. Jay Gerber Professor of Dispute Resolution and Organizations, Professor of Management and Organizations, Director of Kellogg Team and Group Research Center, Northwestern University's Kellogg School of Management, USA

CYNTHIA S. WANG

Executive Director of the Dispute Resolution and Research Center and Clinical Professor of Management and Organizations, Northwestern University's Kellogg School of Management, USA

Elgar Advanced Introductions

 Edward **Elgar**
PUBLISHING

Cheltenham, UK • Northampton, MA, USA

Published by
Edward Elgar Publishing Limited
The Lypiatts
15 Lansdown Road
Cheltenham
Glos GL50 2JA
UK

Edward Elgar Publishing, Inc.
William Pratt House
9 Dewey Court
Northampton
Massachusetts 01060
USA

A catalogue record for this book
is available from the British Library

Library of Congress Control Number: 2022941144

ISBN 978 1 78990 911 1 (cased)
ISBN 978 1 78990 913 5 (paperback)
ISBN 978 1 78990 912 8 (eBook)

Printed and bound in Great Britain by TJ Books Limited, Padstow, Cornwall

We thank Ellen Hampton, Elizabeth Asako Kinase-Leggett, and Vani Sattiraju for their assistance in the preparation of this manuscript.

Contents

About the authors

Leigh Thompson

Leigh Thompson is the J. Jay Gerber Professor of Dispute Resolution at the Kellogg School of Management at Northwestern University. Thompson has published over 100 research articles and books in the areas of negotiation, teamwork, creativity, and group decision making. Some of Thompson's books include: *Negotiating the Sweet Spot: The Art of Leaving Nothing on the Table, Creative Conspiracy: The New Rules of Breakthrough Collaboration, Making the Team: A Guide for Managers, The Mind and Heart of the Negotiator, The Truth about Negotiations, and Stop Spending, Start Managing.*

Thompson teaches MBA, Executive MBA and Executive Education courses in the areas of: Leading High Impact Teams, High Performance Negotiation Skills, Negotiating in a Virtual World, Creativity as a Competitive Edge: Inspiration, Ideation and Implementation, Negotiation Master Class and Constructive Collaboration.

For more information about Dr. Leigh Thompson, visit her website: LeighThompson.com and wiki page: Leigh Thompson.

Cynthia S. Wang

Cynthia S. Wang is the Executive Director of the Dispute Resolution and Research Center and a Clinical Professor of Management and Organizations at Northwestern University's Kellogg School of Management. She has taught negotiations for over 15 years. She has published in top research outlets and her work has received attention from media outlets such as *Time* Magazine and *The New York Times*.

She is an active member in the international academic community, the President of the International Association for Conflict Management, and a Fulbright Scholar. Prior to her academic life, she worked in marketing role managing and consulting for public and private sector organizations.

1 A multi-disciplinary approach

The study of negotiation is a uniquely multi-disciplinary approach. It has roots in several fields including economics, psychology, communication, and labor–management relations. The fact that several disciplines developed extensive theory and empirical research on the topic of negotiation enriches the study of negotiation. The disciplinary roots of negotiation have complemented, rather than competed with one another. It is useful to begin our study of these multi-disciplines by examining the economic roots of negotiation as the field of economics has exerted a large influence on the theoretical and empirical study of negotiation in other disciplines.

1.1 Economic Roots

According to economics, negotiation is a two-party decision-making situation, with the challenge being that the two (or more) parties must make mutual decisions regarding the allocation of scarce resources and do not have identical preferences. The parties have mixed-motives, meaning they want to cooperate so as to reach agreement and avoid a potential costly no-agreement alternative, but their preferences may be in competition. The economic approach to negotiation provides a theory of optimal behavior of how to make choices in light of this mixed-motive situation.

1.1.1 Rationality Assumption

The key principle of economics that undergirds the study of negotiation is the assumption of rationality, which states that people act so as to maximize their utility. This principle of rationality is based on expected utility theory. The utility principle of rationality is often thought to imply that people simply care about money. This is not true. Rationality means

1

people act to maximize their interests, *however they may define their interests*. Interests may include anything people care about, be it monetary gain, career advancement, successful relationships, and peace of mind. For this reason, it is assumed people seek to maximize their *utility* in negotiation, not strictly to maximize their economic *value*. Utility represents the satisfaction a person derives from a particular outcome, not the actual monetary outcome itself.

Another key aspect of the rationality principle is that people's choices should be consistent, such that people's choices should be predictable and follow certain principles. This is an important implication because if people's preferences are inconsistent, it is not possible to evaluate their choices nor predict them. A good example is the principle of transitive choice, which states that if a person prefers x to y, and y over z, then that person should also prefer x over z. If they did not, their preferences would not be transitive and henceforth, violate a key principle of economic utility theory. The rationality principle provides a straightforward method for thinking about decisions and provides a method for choosing among options that produce the best outcome for the negotiator.

1.1.2   Nash's Bargaining Theory

Nash's bargaining theory focuses on how negotiators should divide resources, which involves "a determination of the amount of satisfaction each individual should expect to get from the situation or rather, a determination of how much it should be worth to each of these individuals to have this opportunity to bargain" (Nash, 1950). Nash's theory makes a specific point prediction for the outcome of negotiation, also known as the Nash solution, which specifies the outcome of a negotiation if people behave rationally.

Nash's theory makes several important assumptions in addition to the rationality principle. Nash postulates the settlement (or agreement) point of a negotiation, known as the *Nash solution*, will satisfy the following five axioms: uniqueness, pareto-optimality, symmetry, independence of equivalent utility representations, and independence of irrelevant alternatives.

1.1.2.1 Uniqueness

The uniqueness axiom states that a unique solution exists for each bargaining situation. Simply stated, one, and only one, best solution exists for a given bargaining situation or game.

1.1.2.2 Pareto-Optimality

In many ways, the pareto-optimality assumption is the most important assumption of Nash's theory. The pareto-optimality assumption states that the bargaining process should not yield any outcome both people find less desirable than some other feasible outcome. The pareto-optimality (or efficiency) axiom is the joint rationality assumption (Pareto, 1906). The pareto-optimal frontier is the set of outcomes corresponding to the entire set of agreements that leaves no portion of the total amount of resources available to negotiators unallocated. Formally, a given option, x, is a member of the pareto-optimal frontier if, and only if, no option y exists such that y is preferred to x by at least one party and is at least as good as x for the other party. Stated yet another way, the outcome is pareto-optimal if there does not exist another feasible outcome that would be better for at least one party without hurting the other party.

Options that are not on the pareto-optimal frontier are *dominated*; meaning there exists another viable set of terms that both parties would prefer or which one party would prefer without the loss or value for the other party. Settlements that are dominated by feasible outcomes that both negotiators would prefer instead of their agreed-upon settlement clearly violate the fundamental rationality assumption – the utility principle of maximization. The resolution of any negotiation should be an option from the pareto-efficient set because any other option unnecessarily requires more concessions on the part of one or both negotiators.

It may seem absurd that negotiators would willingly settle for an option that both prefer less than another readily available option, but this happens when negotiators fail to understand the counterparty's preferences.

1.1.2.3 Symmetry

In a symmetric bargaining situation, the two players have exactly the same strategic possibilities and bargaining power. Therefore, neither player has

4 ADVANCED INTRODUCTION TO NEGOTIATION

any reason to accept an agreement that yields a lower payoff than that of the opponent.

Another way of thinking about symmetry is to imagine interchanging the two players. This alteration should not change the outcome. The symmetry principle is often considered to be the fundamental postulate of bargaining theory (Harsanyi, 1962). When parties' utilities are known, the solution to the negotiation problem is straightforward (Nash, 1950). However, players' utilities are usually not known. This uncertainty reduces the usefulness of the symmetry principle. That is, symmetry cannot be achieved if a negotiator has only half of the information (Schelling, 1960).

The pareto-optimality and symmetry axioms uniquely define the agreement points of a symmetrical negotiation situation. The remaining two axioms extend the theory to asymmetrical negotiations in which the bargaining power is asymmetric.

1.1.2.4 Independence of Equivalent Utility Representations

Many utility functions can represent the same preference. Utility functions are behaviorally equivalent if one can be obtained from the other by an order-preserving linear transformation (e.g., by shifting the zero point of the utility scale or by changing the utility unit). A distinguishing feature of the Nash solution outcomes is that it is independent of the exchange rate between two players' utility scales; it is invariant with respect to any fixed weights we might attach to their respective utilities.

The solution to a negotiation situation is not sensitive to positive linear transformations of parties' payoffs because utility is defined on an interval scale. Interval scales, such as temperature, preserve units of measurement but have an arbitrary origin (i.e., zero point) and unit of measurement.

For example, suppose you and a friend are negotiating to divide 100 poker chips. The poker chips are worth $1 each if redeemed by you and worth $1 each if redeemed by your friend. The question is this: How should the two of you divide the poker chips? The Nash solution predicts that the two of you should divide all the chips and not leave any on the table (pareto-optimality principle). Further, the Nash solution predicts that you should receive 50 chips and your friend should receive 50 chips (symmetry principle). So far, the Nash solution sounds fine. Now, suppose the situation is slightly changed. Imagine the chips are worth $1 each if redeemed by you, but they are worth $5 each if redeemed by your friend. The rules of the game do not permit any kind of side payments or renegotiation of redemption values. Now, how should the chips be divided? All we have done is transform your friend's utilities using an order-preserving linear transformation (multiply all their values by 5) while keeping your utilities the same. The Nash solution states that you should still divide the chips 50–50 because your friend's utilities have not changed; rather they are represented by a different, but nevertheless equivalent linear transformation.

Some people have a hard time with this axiom. After all, if you and your friend are really "symmetric," one of you should not come out richer in the deal. But consider the arguments that could be made for one of you receiving a greater share of the chips. One of you could have a seriously ill parent and need the money for medical treatment, one of you might be independently wealthy and not need the money, or one of you could be a foolish spendthrift and not deserve the money. Moreover, there could be a disagreement: One of you regards yourself to be thoughtful and prudent but is regarded as silly and imprudent by the other person. All of these arguments are outside the realm of Nash's theory because they are indeterminate. Dividing resources to achieve monetary equality is as arbitrary as flipping a coin.

But in negotiation, doesn't everything really boil down to dollars? No. In Nash's theory, each person's utility function may be normalized on a scale of 0 to 1, so that his or her "best outcome" = 1 and "worst outcome" = 0. Therefore, because the choices of origin and scale for each person's utility function are unrelated to one another, actual numerical levels have no standing in theory and no comparisons of numerical levels can affect the outcome.

This axiom has serious implications. Permitting the transformation of one player's utilities without any transformation of the other player's utilities destroys the possibility that the outcome should depend on interpersonal utility comparisons. Stated simply, it is meaningless for a person to compare their utility with another person's utility. As we shall see, this axiom will become very important to social scientists. The same logic applies for comparing salaries, the size of offices, or anything else.

Of course, we know that people do engage in interpersonal comparisons of utility! As such, interpersonal comparisons and arguments based on "fairness" are inherently subjective, which leaves no rational method for fair division. And this departure from economic theory spurred the rise of behavioral negotiation theory research, which focuses on how people deviate from the predictions of rational, economic models.

1.1.2.5   *Independence of Irrelevant Alternatives*

The independence of irrelevant alternatives axiom states that the best outcome in a feasible set of outcomes will also be the best outcome in any smaller subset of feasible outcomes which still contains that outcome. For example, a subset of a bargaining situation may be obtained by excluding some of the irrelevant alternatives from the original situation, without excluding the original agreement point itself. The exclusion of irrelevant alternatives does not change the settlement.

The independence of irrelevant alternatives axiom is motivated by the way a negotiation unfolds (Harsanyi, 1990). Through a process of voluntary mutual concessions, the set of possible outcomes under consideration gradually decreases to just those around the eventual agreement point. This axiom asserts the winnowing process does not change the agreement point.

In summary, Nash's theorem states that the unique solution possesses the properties of uniqueness, pareto-optimality, symmetry, independence of equivalent utility representations, and independence of irrelevant alternatives. The Nash solution selects the unique point that maximizes the geometric average (i.e., the product) of the gains available to people as measured against their reservation points (i.e., their "no-agreement" alternatives). For this reason, the Nash solution is also known as the Nash product.

Economic models provide the perfect stage for behavioral researchers to study negotiation. Armed with clear predictions about what people should do if they were indeed rational, social psychologists and behavioral decision researchers can then examine the factors influencing people's behavior in negotiation. Economic models are especially appealing because one of the oft-cited criticisms of social psychology (and other behavioral research) is that the "findings are obvious." If researchers can point to ways people depart from rational models, this is not only surprising (i.e., not obvious), it is important to understand so that research can then turn its focus on how to repair the faulty decision maker.

Now that we have reviewed the key principles of economic theory, we can examine how social psychologists study negotiation behavior.

1.2   Social Psychology

Social psychologists, interested in the study of conflict and how people maintain relationships, conceptualized the problem of negotiation in ways strikingly similar to the work of Nash and von Neumann and Morgenstern. Like economists before them, social psychologists conceptualized parties' interests as reflecting mixed-motives, such that they want to resolve differences and reach agreement, but they do not have identical preferences. The key difference was that social psychologists pioneered methods to empirically study and measure the "bargaining problem," rather than simply outlining a theory of rational behavior. In fact, social psychologists focused on how people consistently violated principles of rationality. Moreover, the focus of social-psychological research was not purely prescriptive (i.e., specifying what people should do), but instead, was primarily descriptive, focusing on what people actually do.

1.2.1   Siegel and Fouraker

One of the first systematic, behavioral studies of negotiation was the research collaboration of Siegel and Fouraker (1960). This collaboration was a true integration of psychology (Siegel) and economics (Fouraker). In their seminal book, Siegel and Fouraker (1960) examined buyer–seller negotiations concerning a hypothetical commodity with real payoffs contingent upon performance. It is worth noting that economists are highly skeptical of research protocols that do not properly incentivize participants, arguing that in absence of meaningful incentives, people's observed behaviors cannot generalize to actual situations containing real incentives. Siegel and Fouraker's studies were carefully conducted with several controls that effectively minimized communication between buyers and sellers, so as to isolate and test the causal impact of certain variables. One of their key findings was that most buyer–seller pairs arrived at settlement prices that produced a 50-50 division of the maximum joint payoff, and variation in prices was reduced as information increased. One of their intriguing, counterintuitive findings was that the member of the bargaining pair who had more information was at a disadvantage because they were quicker to arrive at the equitable offer and were handicapped in subsequent negotiations. Another one of their key contributions was the consideration of negotiators' level of aspiration. Whereas economic theory proposed resistance points to reflect the value of the no-agreement alternative, Siegel and Fouraker focused on the most attractive outcomes a negotiator could strive for. The level of aspiration became a focal point of their research on the bargaining problem.

1.2.2   Kelley

Kelley and his colleagues (Thibaut & Kelley, 1959; Kelley & Thibaut, 1969; Kelley & Schenitzki, 1972) were pivotal in studying what has become contemporary behavioral negotiation research. Kelley's groundbreaking interdependence theory, or social exchange theory (Thibaut & Kelley, 1959) was heavily influenced by the principles of game theory, such that people exchange (negotiate) rewards and costs with one another in a relationship. Kelley used economic terms and made predictions consistent with economic principles of rationality to argue that people seek to maximize good outcomes and minimize costs in relationships. Unlike the economic approaches that preceded social exchange theory, Kelley focused on personal, intimate relationships and argued that marriages and other long-term, intimate relationships could be usefully studied with economic principles.

Kelley broke new ground in a rather obscure 1966 publication that introduced a novel paradigm to study negotiation. Rather than rely on a prisoner's dilemma game with a simple binary choice and complete information, Kelley formulated a more complex task in which two people were each given separate "payoff schedules" (that used points to reflect economic gains) and did not have knowledge of the other party's payoffs (Kelley, 1966). Pairs of people negotiated five issues, and each of the issues had 20 possible alternatives. In this induced-preference paradigm, each party was instructed to act in a way that would maximize one's own payoffs. Yet unbeknownst to the negotiators, there existed a mutually superior (dominant) outcome that both parties preferred over other feasible outcomes. On the surface, it appeared that parties' interests were diametrically opposed; however, one of the parties stood to gain the most points on the second issue; whereas the other party stood to gain the most points on the third and fourth issues. Thus, a pareto-optimal solution entailed settling upon terms that awarded the first player their most important issues and the second player, their most important issues. This method, known as the *induced-preference paradigm*, became the gold standard for the behavioral study of negotiation. Kelley's methodology provided a novel, measurable way to assess pareto-optimality. Kelley's paradigm is still the dominant paradigm used by social scientists as well as practitioner-trainers.

1.2.3   Morley and Stephenson

In their seminal book, *The Social Psychology of Bargaining*, Morley and Stephenson (1977) examined the social-psychological factors that influence the bargaining process. Their book provided a framework and taxonomy for studying negotiation. The key contributions of their research focused on how communication, such as telephone or face-to-face interaction, as well as communication restraints (interruptions) affected negotiation settlements. Unlike Siegel and Fouraker who deliberately constrained the communication between buyers and sellers, Morley and Stephenson examined the language of negotiators using a paradigm rich in communication which allowed parties to communicate without constraints. They developed a coding scheme to code units of language using a technique called the *Conference Process Analysis*. They concluded that the language in negotiations could be identified in terms of "psychological units" and coded. Specifically, they identified three key stages. In the first stage, distributive bargaining, parties test the possible demands, establish criteria for appropriate settlements, assess the power of each side, and evaluate each party's case. In the second stage, problem-solving, parties explore a range of solutions that might satisfy the criteria established at the outset. This stage includes tactical maneuvering, but the key focus is on proposing and evaluating solutions to identified problems. In the final decision-making stage, the parties come to agreement on some terms and explore the implications of their decision. The focus is on reality-checking and assessing the feasibility and implementation of terms that both parties can support. Their focus on language and verbal exchange moved away from a narrow focus on agreed-upon outcomes and toward a new era of research focusing on communication and interaction patterns.

1.2.4 McClintock and van Avermaet

McClintock and van Avermaet (1982) focused on the motivations of parties at the bargaining table and asserted that self-interest (i.e., individual rationality) is not the only goal guiding negotiators' choices at the bargaining table. In this sense, McClintock and van Avermaet's theory represented a significant departure from economic theory, which focused strictly on individual rationality without regard for consideration of the other party's outcomes. McClintock and van Avermaet introduced a model in which negotiators' self-interest is represented on one continuum, ranging from total self-interest on the one extreme (individualism) to a desire to hurt the self on the other extreme (masochism). The other continuum represents the negotiator's concern for the other party, ranging from complete altruism on the one extreme (desire to help the other party) to aggression on the other extreme (desire to hurt the other party). When combined, the circumplex model yielded eight major motivations: individualism, cooperation, competition, altruism, aggression, martyrdom, masochism, and sadomasochism. Of these eight motivations, three are widely studied: individualism (high self-interest), competition (high self-interest and low other-interest), and cooperation (high self-interest and high other-interest).

1.2.5 Deutsch

Morton Deutsch was a pioneer in focusing on the broad topics of justice in conflict (Deutsch, 1973; 1985). In his book, *The Resolution of Conflict*, Deutsch (1973) differentiated between constructive and destructive conflict. Deutsch asserted that conflict could have a beneficial impact on parties and society by setting the stage for a mutually beneficial resolution. Deutsch outlined the factors that could lead parties toward constructive versus destructive conflict, including their values and motivations, as well as their prior relationship and the social environment. Deutsch's focus on constructive and destructive conflict also represented an important departure from economic approaches. Namely, Deutsch argued that parties care not only about economic outcomes received, but also, the method or process used to allocate such outcomes. In this sense, Deutsch expanded the concept of utility to put value on the means or process of conflict and dispute resolution, and not simply on the final outcome.

In his book, *Distributive Justice*, Deutsch (1985) focused on how rewards (and punishments) are allocated. Deutsch considered the principles of equity, equality, and need as systems of justice. Deutsch provided pre-scriptive advice for developing systems of justice.

Extending this framework, Deutsch's students, Allan Lind and Tom Tyler (1988) developed a theory of procedural justice and the specified conditions under which people feel that justice systems are fair. Whereas outcome justice focuses on how resources are allocated amongst parties, procedural justice focuses on the methods or procedures by which scarce resources are allocated. Lind, Tyler and their colleagues argued (and tested) the assumption that people's satisfaction (i.e., the utility they derive) from conflict and negotiation situations is heavily influenced by the methods and procedures used. For example, a key procedural justice factor is the extent to which people are allowed to voice or express their beliefs (Tyler, Rasinski, & Spodick, 1985). This is a significant finding because economic theory strictly focused on the realization of utility in the form of the negotiation outcomes.

1.2.6   Pruitt and Rubin

Dean Pruitt was influenced by the seminal writings of Walton and McKersie (1965) in their work, *A Behavioral Theory of Labor Relations*. Pruitt tossed aside the prisoner's dilemma paradigm and focused on the bargaining problem (as articulated by Kelley, 1966) in which negotiators do not have full information about the other party, but must nevertheless make mutual decisions. Pruitt and Rubin's (1986) dual concern model was a breakthrough theoretical framework that prompted dozens of empirical studies. Like McClintock's circumplex model, Pruitt argued that at any one time, negotiators' behavior was influenced by two "concerns": one reflecting the self and one reflecting the other party. According to the dual concern model, negotiators need both a high concern for the self and a high concern for the other party to reach pareto-optimal agreements. In several studies, Pruitt and his colleagues found that pareto-optimal agree-ments were usually attained only when parties embraced dual concerns (i.e., a concern for the self and a concern about the other party).

Moreover, in several dozen studies, Pruitt and his colleagues inde-pendently manipulated a negotiator's concern for the self and a negotia-tor's concern for the other party. Concern for the self was manipulated (in many cases) by providing a particular goal or aspiration that the negotia-tor needed to achieve, also known as a resistance to yielding (Ben-Yoav &

Pruitt, 1984). Concern for the other party was manipulated (among other methods) by informing negotiators that they should expect to interact with the other party in the future. According to the dual concern model, the expectation of future interaction would motivate negotiators to care about the other party. The results from these studies provided support from the dual concern model (see DeDreu, Weingart, & Kwon, 2000, for a meta-analysis).

Another method to induce a concern for the self was to make negotiators accountable to a constituency. Negotiators are accountable to their constituents when their constituents can reward or punish them for their performance (Ben-Yoav & Pruitt, 1984). Indeed, negotiators who were accountable (versus not accountable) to constituents and who did not expect to interact with the other party in the future reached lower joint profits (non pareto-optimal solutions), presumably because their concern for the self, but not the other, was high. However, negotiators who were accountable to constituents (high self-concern) and who expected to interact with the other party in the future (high other-concern) attained higher joint outcomes.

1.3 Labor Relations and Management

In this section, we examine models of negotiation that do not represent classic economic game theory, but instead are focused on how to advise managers in the throes of negotiation. These researchers, many of whom were economists, realized that people do not follow principles of rationality. Moreover, they turned their focus not just to game theoretical predictions based upon rationality, but also to providing strategic advice and best practices for the negotiator. Unlike the pure economic theory, the researchers in this field used actual, as well as illustrative negotiation situations and scenarios, to make their points.

1.3.1 Walton and McKersie

Walton and McKersie's seminal book, *A Behavioral Theory of Labor Negotiations* (1965), elegantly did several things. First, Walton and McKersie clearly delineated distributive (i.e., zero-sum) versus integrative (i.e., leveraging differences in opinions and forecasts) negotiation. Second, they pointed to the importance of *attitudinal structuring*, whereby they meant the parties to a negotiation might try to influence and persuade one another, such as through argumentation, wherein one party may try to change the utility function of the other party. Finally, their book focused on navigating internal negotiation situations. Many of their illustrative examples focused on labor–management situations in which strike was a behavioral option.

In a follow-up book, *Strategic Negotiations*, Walton, Cutcher-Gershenfeld, and McKersie (1994) outlined a theory of advice for the negotiator and used illustrative business, labor, and political examples to point the manager toward integrative agreements. Like others in the labor and management fields, Walton and colleagues set aside the strict tenets of game-theory language (e.g., Nash equilibrium, pareto-optimality) and introduced the reader to more readily understandable and applied concepts that focused on how to achieve joint gains.

1.3.2   Raiffa

Howard Raiffa, a game theorist, had a unique gift for writing powerfully and clearly using examples that elegantly illustrated otherwise hard-to-follow concepts. In his seminal book, *The Art and Science of Negotiation* (1982), Raiffa did three key things. First, Raiffa neatly distinguished prescriptive versus descriptive research, aptly noting that prescriptive research is largely the domain of economists, whereas descriptive research is largely the domain of social scientists and psychologists. Realizing that the two camps may never speak to one another, Raiffa introduced a third purpose of research, which he defined as "asymmetric descriptive prescriptive research." Raiffa explained that given people may not behave in accordance with economic models, it is important to understand their shortcomings and provide methods to help them, lest they experience economic and psychological loss.

A second major implication of Raiffa's treatise was the highly practical advice, presented in the form of the strategies he offered. Raiffa provided detailed descriptions of captivating business and political negotiations, ranging from city legislatures to the Panama Canal negotiations. For each example, Raiffa provided a detailed examination and treatment of the conflict, and a non-obvious solution that clearly pointed to the fact that by surfacing information, particularly regarding parties' interests, elegant solutions were possible. One of Raiffa's most powerful prescriptions involved risk-sharing and insecure contracts in which parties could fashion integrative agreements by leveraging their differing opinions and forecasts.

A third key contribution of Raiffa's seminal book was the chapter (Chapter 5, "Negotiation Analysis") in which he provided a veritable classification of conflict types. In this chapter, Raiffa posed several questions for the manager–practitioner to consider, including: "are the negotiations long-term or one-off?"; "are there linkage effects?"; and "are side deals permitted?" These questions not only served as organizing devices for practical advice, but also spurred the development of behavioral research investigations.

1.3.3   Fisher and Ury

You will be hard-pressed to find a manager or business student who has not heard of *Getting to Yes* and likely has a well-worn copy at the top of their bookcase. In their seminal paperback book, *Getting to Yes*, Roger Fisher and William Ury (1981) synthesized decades of arcane economic theory in the form of practical advice for the busy manager–negotiator. They smartly tossed aside the cumbersome terms, "no-agreement alternative" and "CLalt" and substituted the catchy acronym, "BATNA" (Best Alternative To a Negotiated Agreement). Using powerful, yet relatable stories and situations, sometimes only a few sentences long, Fisher and Ury invited the manager into the world of win–win negotiation. This single book marked the explosion of research and practical application of negotiation (Thompson & Leonardelli, 2004).

1.3.4   Lax and Sebenius

In their book, *The Manager as Negotiator*, Lax and Sebenius (1986) deftly weaved together the insights of economics and psychology in the form of practical advice. Lax and Sebenius introduced the "negotiator's dilemma" which they described as the fact that revealing information about one's interests may maximize joint gains (and ensure a pareto-optimal outcome) but put the negotiator at a strategic disadvantage. They focused intently on the subject of maximizing joint gains (a concept analogous to the pareto-optimality axiom). Through incisive analysis of actual negotiation situations, Lax and Sebenius focused on how differences among parties pave the way toward integrative agreements.

1.4   Summary

The theoretical and empirical study of negotiation has been influenced and shaped by several fields, most notably economics, psychology, and labor–management relations. These different fields have collaborated much more than they have competed with one another. The study of negotiation is particularly rich because it has been shaped by powerful theories of economics and has been robustly empirically studied by psychologists (as well as experimental economists). In many ways, one of the great contributions of management and labor relations theorists has been one of acknowledging the compelling prescriptive theory, but simultaneously gently noting the actual behavior of people may depart from these prescriptive theories. Psychologists, like Kelley, ingeniously created a methodology to study negotiation behavior which is still used more than a half-a-century later.

2 Core concepts

Despite the interdisciplinary history of negotiation, the core concepts in each of the sub-fields are nearly identical, allowing scholars across disciplines to collaborate and use similar methods. However, the core concepts are known by different names in the various disciplines, which can create potential confusion for researchers and practitioners of negotiation. Thus, it is worthwhile outlining these concepts and core terms. In this chapter, we identify key terms, concepts, and constructs used to study negotiation. These constructs have been operationalized in different ways across research disciplines.

2.1 Prescriptive versus Descriptive Models

Prescriptive models, such as that outlined by Nash and other economists, focus on how negotiators *should* behave if they were rational in their choices. By rational, we mean of course, adhering to the five key principles of rationality as articulated by Nash (in Chapter 1). Thus, prescriptive models focus on how negotiators ideally make choices. Prescriptive models are theoretical and are not intended to be empirically tested, as the mathematical model is the "proof" of the theorem.

Conversely, descriptive models, such as those outlined by Kelley and many other social psychologists, focus on how negotiators actually behave. Descriptive models are designed to be empirically tested through laboratory and field experimentation. Laboratory experimentation typically allows for causal testing of different factors. Social psychologists and behavioral researchers do not believe that people behave in accordance with the predictions of game theoretic models. As we shall see, many people do not make choices consistent with what rational models might predict.

Raiffa aptly christened a third type of model, the "asymmetrically prescriptive/descriptive" approach. Because people often fail to act in accordance with the prescriptions of economic models, Raiffa argued that it is more useful to advise negotiators on how they should act based on how the other party will likely act. Thus, Raiffa's asymmetrically prescriptive/descriptive approach acknowledges that acting in accordance with rational models can best optimize the negotiator's interests, but that people do not always behave in ways consistent with that ideal. Therefore, behavioral research is best served by providing advice for negotiators.

2.2   Distributive and Integrative Negotiation

The most fundamental distinction in negotiation research is that between distributive versus integrative negotiation. *Distributive* negotiation focuses on how parties divide and allocate resources among them. Deutsch's theory of distributive justice, which describes how the distribution of resources affect the parties at the table is an example (Deutsch, 1985). *Integrative* negotiation refers to how parties enlarge the available resources by finding the pareto-optimal frontier. Kelley's (1966) classroom study is an example of integrative negotiation in which some feasible settlements are preferred by both parties and dominate other settlements. One important point to keep in mind is that all negotiations have a distributive element, but not all negotiation situations have an integrative element. Practically speaking, no matter how large negotiators make the "pie of mutual gains," they must ultimately divide those resources.

2.2.1   Fixed- and Variable-Sum Games

Management and behavioral research scholars most commonly use the language of distributive and integrative negotiations, whereas game theorists instead use the language of fixed- and variable-sum games. *Fixed-sum* games refer to the fact that some negotiations involve the division of a fixed-sum of resources (also known as zero-sum). Conversely, *variable-sum* games contain potential for some outcomes to be more mutually beneficial than others. The prisoner's dilemma is an example of a variable-sum game with complete information because the payoff matrix is available to both parties and mutual cooperation yields higher joint gains than does mutual defection.

Whereas game theory's concepts of "fixed" and "variable" sum games strictly refer to the nature of parties' incentives relative to one another, the constructs of "distributive" and "integrative" negotiation also refer to the behaviors of negotiators (as well as the nature of their incentives). In other words, behavioral negotiation researchers often use "distributive" and "integrative" to describe the behavior of negotiators. Most commonly, "distributive" behaviors refer to making aggressive offers, refusing to concede, and so on, whereas "integrative" behaviors refer to revealing interests, suggesting options, and focusing on mutual interests.

2.2.2   Creating and Claiming Value

When we consider the behavioral usage of "distributive" and "integrative" negotiation, another pair of closely related terms is that of "claiming" and "creating" value (Lax & Sebenius, 1986). In this context, *claiming* refers to how negotiators compete with one another; whereas *creating* refers to how negotiators attempt to collaborate with one another given that mutual agreement is likely to be superior to exercising one's no-agreement alternatives. Lax and Sebenius refer to claiming and creating as the "mixed-motive" nature of negotiation, such that parties want to cooperate so as to reach agreement, but they know that their preferences may be in competition. This tension forms the "negotiator's dilemma."

2.2.3   Cooperation and Competition

Whereas we focus on distributive and integrative negotiation to refer to behaviors and motives, these constructs are also closely aligned with the motives of competition and cooperation. When social scientists and behavioral researchers began to use the terms, distributive/claiming/competitive (and integrative/creating/cooperative) to refer to behaviors and motives, this spurred new research questions (Bottom & Studt, 1993). Such constructs could be manipulated (via incentives and instructions) and treated as causal factors; they could also be measured as dependent variables. For example, Bazerman, Magliozzi, and Neale (1985) demonstrated that positively framed negotiators acted more cooperatively than did negatively framed negotiators.

2.2.4 Cooperative versus Non-Cooperative Negotiations

Even more potentially confusing for the young scholar is the treatment of "cooperative" and "non-cooperative" games by economists. According to Nash (1951) there are two types of negotiations: cooperative games (situations) and non-cooperative games. It is important to note that Nash was *not* referring to negotiators' motives (remember, Nash assumes rationality). Instead, Nash was referring to the nature of the game. Negotiations in which people voluntarily reach agreement, such as when a buyer agrees to pay a seller for a good or service or when an employee willingly accepts an offer made by an employer is known as a cooperative game (even though parties may behave competitively). Conversely, negotiations in which people simultaneously make one of two choices, to cooperate or compete, are known as non-cooperative games. The most well-known non-cooperative game is the prisoner's dilemma. Most behavioral researchers, however, have focused on cooperative games, such as buyer–seller negotiations, employee–employer negotiations, labor–management negotiations, and so on. Kelley's (1966) classroom study of negotiation is an example of a cooperative game because parties mutually agree to outcomes.

2.3   No-Agreement Alternative

An essential concept in the study of negotiation is the point at which a negotiator is best advised to not willingly accept the settlement terms offered by the other party but instead, walk away from the table. This point is colloquially referred to as a negotiator's "bottom line" and is meant to express the point at which accepting terms would result in less utility than pursuing an alternative option.

Perhaps no other construct has been christened with as many variant terms as the negotiator's *no-agreement alternative*. Whereas there are nuances to the various terms, they all share a similar theme, rationally speaking, negotiators should (eventually) accept proposals that are better than their no-agreement alternative and reject proposals that are inferior to their no-agreement alternative.

2.3.1   Indifference Point

Economists typically use the term *indifference point* to refer to the precise point that defines whether a given settlement option is superior or inferior to the negotiator's walk-away value. The indifference point refers to the precise point at which a negotiator would be indifferent between settlement and walking away from the table.

2.3.2   Resistance Point

Walton and McKersie (1965) used the term *resistance point* to refer to the point at which negotiators prefer to walk away from the table rather than settle. Walton and McKersie used a labor–management negotiation example to illustrate the resistance point idea, arguing that the negotiator whose alternative to agreement is to declare a strike is best served to determine that point well in advance of negotiations to guide their behavior at the bargaining table. According to Walton and McKersie, the negotiator's resistance point is determined by three considerations: (1) the lowest estimate of what is needed; (2) the most pessimistic assumptions about what is possible; and (3) the least favorable assumptions about one's own bargaining skill relative to the opposition.

2.3.3   Reservation Price or Reservation Point

Raiffa (1982) introduced the terms, *reservation price* and *reservation point* to refer to the negotiator's walk-away point. Reservation price or reservation point is essentially the same concept as resistance point. Like Lax and Sebenius' resistance point construct, the negotiator's reservation point is a specific point that is determined by the utility of the negotiator's alternatives.

2.3.4   CLalt (Comparison Level for Alternatives)

Psychologists Harold Kelley and John Thibaut used the term, *CLalt,* borrowed from their interdependence theory (Kelley & Thibaut, 1969) to signal the point at which a person has alternatives (outside of the relationship) that are considered superior to a given settlement. CLalt refers to a person's *comparison level for alternatives.* Whereas resistance point and reservation point are highly specific and refer to a particular outside option, CLalt referred to a generalized perception, developed by the negotiator of what would be the likely outcome that could be obtained by exiting the current relationship and entering a different relationship. CLalt refers to the lowest level of outcomes in a current relationship that an individual finds acceptable in light of outcomes obtainable in a different relationship. Thus, CLalt is influenced not only by the attractiveness of alternative relationships, but also by the option of non-involvement with the current relationship. Moreover, CLalt influences feelings of dependence, or the level to which a person feels reliant on the current relationship.

2.3.5   B.A.T.N.A. (or *BATNA*)

In 1981, Fisher and Ury introduced the acronym, BATNA (Best Alternative to a Negotiated Agreement), that became the gold standard term used by researchers and practitioners alike. Short, catchy, memorable, and chock-full of captivating examples, Fisher and Ury's *Getting to Yes* (1981) guided the manager–negotiator through the thought process of when to agree to a particular deal versus take one's battle elsewhere. The acronym, BATNA, stuck – in the minds of practitioners, managers, and researchers alike.

It is important to realize that the term, BATNA, refers to a specific, outside-the-relationship option that is available to a negotiator. BATNA and CLalt are analogous. However, a negotiator's BATNA is not the same as the negotiator's reservation price (or resistance point). Think of a BATNA as the course of action the negotiator will take if the current deal falls through or is otherwise eliminated. Think of a reservation price as the very lowest price that a seller would accept (or the very highest price that a buyer would offer) before walking away from the table and exercising their BATNA. Thus, a BATNA is a course of action a negotiator takes *outside* of a given negotiation; whereas a reservation price is the most unattractive terms a negotiator would agree to *within* a given negotiation. A negotiator's reservation point is then, a quantification of their BATNA.

2.4   Settlement Range

The settlement range is the area between parties' reservation points or resistance points. The settlement range can be positive, negative, or even a single point. If the settlement range is positive, it is in both parties' interests to reach a settlement point; if the settlement range is negative (or non-existent), parties should not reach a deal and exercise their no-agreement alternatives.

2.4.1   ZOPA (Zone of Possible Agreement)

The term ZOPA (zone of possible agreement) refers to the distance between the buyer's reservation point and the seller's reservation point and represents a range, which can be positive (when the buyer and seller are both better off by reaching mutual agreement than walking away); or negative (when the buyer and seller have outside alternatives they find more attractive than reaching agreement). The ZOPA is positive when the buyer is willing to pay more than the least the seller will accept. The ZOPA is negative when the most the buyer is willing to pay is less than the very lowest the seller is willing to accept.

2.5   Target Point

Negotiators do not settle for the first available terms that are better than their respective reservation points. In keeping with the axioms of rational utility theory, negotiators seek to attain the most favorable settlement possible. An essential concept for the study of negotiation is a negotiator's target point. Also known as a negotiator's goal, comparison level (CL) and aspiration, these terms commonly refer to the most ideal terms in the eyes of the negotiator.

Walton and McKersie (1965) used the term, target point, when they advised negotiators to prepare a decision rule, arguing that negotiations are not one-shot decision-making situations, but instead involve a series of decisions interspersed with performance activities and goal strivings. Walton and McKersie focused carefully on the language that negotiators use to present their goal strivings (aka target points), noting that "*I hope*"; "*I'd be happy with…*"; and "*I must have*" refer to different points on the bargaining spectrum. Walton and McKersie summarized that a negotiator's target point represents a consideration of three things: their highest estimate of what is needed, their most optimistic assumptions, and their most favorable assumptions about their own bargaining skill relative to the opponent.

2.5.1   Level of Aspiration

Siegel and Fouraker (1960) used the term, level of aspiration, to refer to the most favorable terms a negotiator realistically hopes to get. Level-of-aspiration (LOA) theory specifies that it is to a negotiator's advantage to be tough. LOA theory assumes that concessions (i.e., reductions from an initial, opening offer) are a function of a negotiator's aspiration level and that aspirations are subject to manipulation by the counterparty. Specifically, if the counterparty adopts a tough stance (assertive opening offer and few concessions), the negotiator's aspirations will decrease, while a conciliatory (soft) stance will increase a negotiator's aspirations. The key prediction of LOA is that tougher stances (more extreme opening offers, followed by few concessions) will extract larger concessions from the opponent.

2.5.2   Goals

Behavioral scientists quickly started to inform their predictions about negotiator behavior by studying the large literature on goal setting (Locke & Latham, 1990). One of the central tenets of goal-setting theory is that a negotiator is best served by having a specific, difficult goal. For example, Neale and Bazerman (1985) found that negotiators who set specific, difficult goals performed better in terms of claiming resources than negotiators with non-specific or easy goals. Moreover, focusing on one's target (or goal) can negate the first offer effect (i.e., anchoring effect) on outcomes (Galinsky & Mussweiler, 2001).

2.5.3   CL (Comparison Level)

Just as Kelley and Thibaut used the term, *CLalt* to refer to a person's alternatives outside the current relationship, Kelley used the term, *CL* (comparison level) to refer to what a person expects and desires within a relationship. According to Kelley, a negotiator's CL reflects the benefits they have come to expect to receive by continuing to invest in a given relationship.

2.6   Issues and Alternatives

The *issues* are the resources to be allocated or the considerations to be negotiated. The *alternatives* are the options within each issue. For example, in a salary negotiation; the "issues" may include base salary, signing bonus, vacation days, stock options, starting date, and so on. The "alternatives" for starting date may include dates ranging from May 1 to July 1. Together, the issues and alternatives form the "issue mix." Note that used in this sense, "alternatives" do not refer to one's no-agreement alternative.

2.6.1   Preferences and Priorities

The negotiators are expected to have preferences regarding the issue mix and priorities across the issues. For example, a given negotiator may prefer to have a later starting date (preference) but salary may be a vastly higher priority than their preferred starting date.

2.7   Opening Offers

When we consider how to strategically advise the negotiator there are two fundamental questions: (1) is it advisable to be the first to make an offer; and (2) what should that offer be? In a non-cooperative game (such as a prisoner's dilemma), there are no back-and-forth offers because the parties make their choices simultaneously. However, in a cooperative negotiation that has incomplete information (such that parties only know their own utilities, and not that of the other), the question of who should make the opening offer is fraught with debate. Folklore suggests that negotiators are best served to not make the opening offer and let the other person make the offer, presumably in the hopes that the opponent does not ask for enough (seller) or offers a very attractive price (buyer). However, much empirical research suggests that negotiators who make the first offer have an advantage, due to the anchoring effect (Galinsky & Mussweiler, 2001).

2.7.1   Anchoring

Decades of research on two-party negotiation with incomplete information suggest that in general, the negotiator who makes the first offer has an advantage. The key reason for this advantage is what is known as the anchoring effect (Tversky & Kahneman, 1974). According to the anchoring and adjustment effect, the first set of terms exerts a powerful effect on subsequent judgments, such that people fail to make sufficient adjustments once they have been exposed to an anchor (Sherif, Taub, & Hovland, 1958). The anchoring effect is so powerful that it influences judgment even when the anchor is quite arbitrary. For example, in one investigation, negotiators were asked to make estimates of how many African countries were in the United Nations (Tversky & Kahneman, 1974). Prior to making a judgment (guess), a roulette wheel was spun in front of them landing on either a large or small number. Even though everyone realized that the roulette wheel is a game of chance and therefore should not influence their judgment, there was a powerful anchoring effect such that estimates were greater when the arbitrary number was high and much lower estimates when the arbitrary number was low.

2.7.1.1   *Anchoring Information Model*

According to the AIM (Anchoring Information Model), the question of whether it is advisable for negotiators to make an opening offer or induce one from the opposing party depends on information symmetry (Loschelder, Trotschel, Swaab, Friese, & Galinsky, 2016; Maaravi & Levy, 2017). When information is symmetic, negotiators are best advised to make the first offer so that they may benefit from the psychological anchoring effect. However, in situations characterized by information asymmetry, negotiators are advised to prompt the counterparty to make the first offer. The key logic is that the unprepared negotiator may make a too-generous opening offer and the under-prepared opponent may fail to anchor sufficiently.

2.7.2   Ideal Opening Offer

Thus far, we've wrestled with the question of whether negotiators are best advised to make the first offer or induce one from the other party. Another question is once a negotiator has determined it is wise to make an opening offer, how aggressive should it be? At first blush, it would seem that an extremely aggressive opening offer might have the most significant anchoring effect. However, extreme offers are likely to be rejected and sour the negotiation process. For example, in traditional arbitration, the custom is for the third-party arbitrator to propose a settlement that is midway between the final two settlement proposals by the parties in conflict. However, this incentivizes parties to make extremely aggressive final offers, which dramatically decreases the likelihood of mutual settlement (Farber, 1980). Thus, extreme offers create a chilling effect by reducing the likelihood of mutual settlement (Schweinsberg, Ku, Wang, & Pillutla, 2012).

For this reason, negotiators are best served to make an offer that is on or near or slightly outside what they perceive to be the counterparty's reservation price. By definition, such offers are not insulting (because they are in the ZOPA), however, the negotiator ideally does not give up any part of the ZOPA to the other party (Myerson, 1991a; 1991b).

2.7.3   Chilling Effect

In many cases, negotiators hedge their uncertainty about the other party's reservation price and set a too-aggressive goal. They often reason that an aggressive goal might serve as a powerful anchor. However, when negotiators make an aggressive offer that is outside the ZOPA, this can lead to the chilling effect, leading parties to risk a no-agreement alternative and the negotiation loses momentum (Harris & Carnevale, 1990).

2.7.4   Winner's Curse

One risk that negotiators take when developing a reservation price is that their reservation price acts as a psychological anchor and they set a too-conservative target point. In the case where a negotiator's first offer is too generous and is immediately accepted by the other party, this results in the winner's curse (Thaler, 1992). The winner's curse refers to the fact that a negotiator has secured a very quick agreement from the opposing party, but the fact that the opposing party did not resist at all or counteroffer clearly suggests that the opening offer was not sufficiently aggressive.

2.7.5   Counteroffers

A negotiator who has received an offer from the opponent is best advised to counteroffer and resist accepting the first set of terms. The anchoring effect is quite powerful, such that people are often unaware of how their own estimates are influenced by anchors (Galinsky, Seiden, Kim, & Medvec, 2002).

2.7.6   Point versus Range Offers

A key question is whether a negotiator is best served by making a precise, "point" offer or stating a "range." Whereas a range might signal flexibility, thus allowing a negotiator to hedge, it may not serve to be as an effective an anchor as a point offer. Worse yet, the receiving party may only focus on the lower part of the range. For these reasons, point offers are often more effective with one key exception. One study examined the effectiveness three types of range offers: bracketing-, backdown-, and bolstering-range offers. Bracketing-range offers surround a negotiator's target point; backdown ranges are offers that present a range with the highest number being the negotiator's target; and bolstering-range offers present a range, with the lowest number being the negotiator's target (Ames & Mason, 2015). Not surprisingly, bolstering-range offers were the most effective, followed by point and bracketing-range offers; backdown-range offers led to the lowest outcomes for negotiators.

2.7.7   Precise versus Round Numbers as Opening Offers

People habitually use round numbers as a first offer in negotiation (e.g., $5000 for a used car). However, precise anchors (e.g., $4885) are more effective than are round ones when making a first offer. Indeed, counterparties respond more aggressively to round numbers than precise numbers (Mason, Lee, Wiley, & Ames, 2013). Negotiators who make precise offers are viewed as having more information than negotiators who make round offers. The impact of precise offers is due to the fact that the sender appears as more competent (Loschelder, Friese, & Trotschel, 2017). When devising a precise offer, it is important to consider how precision affects the proposer as well as the recipient. Greater precision by the proposer can enhance the anchoring effect in the recipient, even when the offer that the proposer makes is less extreme. Stated another way, proposers who open with a precise, but less extreme offer would still likely claim an equally large share of the ZOPA as they would have if they had opened with a less precise, but more extreme offer.

It is worth noting that offers can actually be too precise, particularly when the recipient is an expert and likely to question the offer. For this reason, greater precision works when the recipient is an amateur, but can backfire when the recipient is an expert (Loschelder, Trotschel, Swaab, Friese, & Galinsky, 2016). The negative (backfiring) effect occurs when the proposer failed to provide a rationale that was legitimate in the eyes of the expert recipient.

2.7.8   Early versus Late Opening Offer

Independent of the question of who makes the first offer is the question of how early into the process of negotiation to present one's opening offer. This raises the question of timing. For example, some negotiations involve the exchange of pleasantries and other conversation before offers are tendered; in other negotiations, people immediately initiate a volley of offers. Late first offers are more likely to lead to integrative agreements that meet both parties' interests, as compared to early first offers – even when controlling for the overall duration of the negotiation. This is because late first offers allow negotiators to learn about the counterparty's interests (Sinaceur, Maddux, Vasiljevic, Nuckel, & Galinsky, 2013).

2.8   Persuasion

2.8.1   Attitudinal Structuring

Attitudinal structuring refers to attempts by negotiators to revise the counterparties' interests, valuations for issues, and preferences (e.g., "your car is not worth as much as you think"). Attitudinal structuring also refers to attempts by negotiators to induce their opponent to believe that their own BATNA is more attractive than it actually is and simultaneously convince the opponent that their BATNA is less attractive or less likely.

2.8.2   Disparagement versus Constraint Rationales

One investigation examined two types of rationales that negotiators made during negotiation (Lee & Ames, 2017). Constraint rationales refer to one's own limited resources (e.g., "*I can't pay more ...*"). In contrast, disparagement rationales critique the negotiated object or service (e.g., "*It's not worth more ...*"). Negotiators who highlighted their own constraints were more successful than negotiators who argued down the value of an item. Constraint rationales signal a negotiator's limits and are therefore more believable. Moreover, constraint rationales are less likely to insult the counterparty.

2.9   Concessions

It is rare that negotiations will end with parties accepting the first offer or counteroffer. Instead, there is likely to be a back-and-forth interchange of offers and counteroffers. Raiffa refers to this as the "dance of negotiation" (Raiffa, 1982).

Concession reciprocity refers to the tendency of negotiators to reciprocate concessions. Concession aversion refers to the tendency for some negotiators to be disinclined to make concessions. Negotiators show stronger concession aversion and ultimately claim more value when negotiation proposals are framed to highlight their own, rather than the counterparties' resources (Trotschel, Loschelder, Hohne, & Majer, 2015). Specifically, proposal-senders show greater concession aversion when they offer their own resources (versus requesting the counterparty's resources) in both buyer and seller negotiations. The opposite is true for recipients: recipients show stronger concession aversion when receiving requests rather than offers.

2.9.1   Concession Pattern

Unilateral concessions are concessions made by one party; in contrast, bilateral concessions are concessions made by both sides. Many negotiators make what we call premature concessions – they make more than one concession in a row before the other party responds or counteroffers (Thompson & Leonardelli, 2004). Negotiators who make fewer and smaller concessions maximize their ability to claim a larger share of the ZOPA, compared to those who make larger and more frequent concessions (Siegel & Fouraker, 1960; Yukl, 1974).

Concessions often follow a quid pro quo pattern, meaning that negotiators engage in a back-and-forth exchange of concessions. However, negotiators should not offer more than a single concession at a time to the counterparty.

Most researchers agree that negotiators are best advised to make concessions in a quid pro quo fashion. However, the relative magnitude of each concession is important to consider. Making a series of decreasing concessions, in which a negotiator's concessions become progressively smaller and smaller over time is advisable. In a series of studies, three types of concession patterns were examined: decreasing (such that each successive concession is smaller than the previous one); constant (each concession decreases by the same magnitude); and a single concession that represents a large decrease (Tey, Schaerer, Madan, & Swaab, 2021). Negotiators who followed the decreasing concession strategy attained the most favorable outcomes, in terms of securing an agreement from the counterparty that gave them more of the ZOPA. In some of the research studies, the concession strategy was examined as a dependent variable (rather than a manipulated strategy) and it was revealed that most negotiators (94%) do not naturally use the decreasing concession strategy despite the fact that it would lead to the most favorable outcomes. The reason why the decreasing concession strategy is effective in leading negotiators to claim a larger share of the ZOPA is that it influences the counterparty's perceptions of the concession-maker's reservation price. Stated another way, when the negotiator (Party A) makes decreasing concessions, the counterparty (Party B) believes that Party A has a more favorable reservation price, than when Party A uses a steady or single concession strategy. For this reason, it is important to consider how a negotiator (Party B) should respond when receiving a string of decreasing concessions from Party A. In this case, negotiators can protect themself against the deleterious effects of decreasing concession by thinking of the target (aspiration) prior to negotiation (Tey, Schaerer, Madan, & Swaab, 2021).

2.9.2   Magnitude of Concessions

Even though negotiators may make concessions in a back-and-forth method, this exchange does not say anything about the size of concessions made by each party. Thus, another consideration when making concessions is to determine how much to concede. The usual measure of a concession is the amount reduced or added (depending upon whether one is a seller or buyer) from one's previous offer. It is unwise to make consistently greater concessions than the counterparty. Moreover, making concessions may not have the desired effect. Negotiators who make large concessions may lose credibility and have the unintended effect of making the other party less willing to concede.

Thus, many prescriptive approaches advise negotiators to match the concession magnitude of the counterparty or make concessions that are slightly smaller in magnitude. Each successive concession should be smaller in magnitude than the previous concessions. Negotiators can signal that they are getting near their reservation point by reducing the size of their concessions. It is far better to make a large number of small concessions than a small number of large concessions.

2.9.3   GRIT

The graduated reduction in tension (GRIT) model is a method in which parties avoid escalating conflict and move toward mutual settlement within the bargaining zone (Osgood, 1962). The GRIT model, based on the reciprocity principle, calls for one party to make a concession and invites the other party to reciprocate by making a concession. The concession offered by the first party is significant, but not so much that the offering party is tremendously disadvantaged if the counterparty fails to reciprocate.

One study examined the degree of concessions made by negotiators over different points in the negotiation process (e.g., early on versus later; Hilty & Carnevale, 1993). Two types of concession patterns were compared: black-hat/white-hat (BH/WH) negotiators and white-hat/black-hat (WH/BH) negotiators. BH/WH negotiators began with a tough stance, made few early concessions, and later made larger concessions. WH/BH negotiators did the opposite: they began with generous concessions and then became tough and unyielding. The BH/WH concession strategy proved to be more effective than the WH/BH strategy in eliciting concessions from the counterparty. The BH-turned-WH sets up a favorable contrast for the receiver. The person who has been dealing with the BH feels relieved to now be dealing with the WH.

2.9.4   Timing of Concessions

The timing of concessions refers to whether they are immediate, gradual, or delayed (Kwon & Weingart, 2004). In an analysis of buyer–seller negotiations, sellers who made immediate concessions received the most negative reaction from the buyer, who showed the least satisfaction and evaluated the object of sale most negatively. In contrast, when the seller made gradual concessions, the buyer's reaction was most positive, with high satisfaction.

2.10   Empirical Paradigms

Social psychologists were key in developing empirical paradigms to examine whether negotiation parties were able to reach pareto-optimal solutions.

2.10.1   Induced-Preference Paradigm

The induced-preference paradigm provides a method for studying (and measuring) negotiation behavior and outcomes. Rather than measuring people's actual preferences (do they really like chocolate more than vanilla?), in the induced-preference paradigm, negotiators are given a payoff schedule (or set of utilities) and instructed to maximize their own interests. This is typically achieved by providing them with monetary (or other) incentives. It is for this reason that economists are highly skeptical about empirical research that does not adequately incentivize players to maximize their (induced) utilities. Thus, many induced-preference paradigms use real incentives (i.e., cash payments and tickets to cash lotteries) as prizes for achieved outcomes.

Kelley (1966) was one of the first researchers to use the induced-preference paradigm in his study of "classroom behavior." In this particular study, pairs of people had to negotiate five sets of terms. Each party to the negotiation was given a list of five columns that specified their payoffs given a set of terms. One of the key features of this method was the parties' interests (utilities) were not completely opposed. Thus, the negotiation was not a fixed-sum (or zero-sum) game; it was a variable-sum game.

Decades later, Pruitt and his colleagues further developed the induced-preference paradigm and used a three-issue game depicted by nine options for each issue, simply labeled as A, B, C, … (Pruitt & Lewis, 1975). The optimal solution for both players was to agree upon A, E, I (A for the first issue, which was most important to player 1, the middle term for the second issue, and I for the third issue which was most important to player 2). Most players naïvely assumed that their interests were diametrically opposed and thus, E, E, E was a common, yet pareto-inefficient solution.

Thompson (and her colleagues) further embellished the induced-preference paradigm by providing a more meaningful context than simply using alpha-numeric numbers. For example, in one investigation, Thompson and Hastie (1990) created an 8-issue negotiation with 5-alternatives for each issue concerning a "new car." Rather than negotiating abstract letters (e.g., "a, b, c"), Thompson's paradigm labeled each issue – alternative (e.g., $5000, $4000, … $2000; and 6 months, 9 months, 12 months (warranty)). Unbeknownst to negotiators was the possibility for a pareto-optimal solution.

2.11   Dependent Variables

There are several dependent variables that are relevant in the study of negotiation. Broadly speaking, dependent variables include outcome measures, process measures, and subjective measures.

Outcome measures include: the extent to which negotiators reach pareto-optimal agreements, the attainment of mutual gains, the individual gains (profits) of each party, and the difference between party 1 and party 2's outcome. Behavioral economists rarely measure pareto-optimally and instead use a simpler method, known as "joint gains" or "joint profit," which is a sum of both parties' outcomes. Higher joint outcomes are considered to be integrative agreements that have maximized both parties' utilities.

Process measures include: analysis of the communication exchange between parties, which often requires recording, transcribing, and coding negotiators' communication and conversation. This can be done at the conversational turn level; and it can be done in terms of the content level, such that on any given conversational turn, a negotiator might say several content-worthy things (Siegel & Fouraker, 1960; Brett, Shapiro, & Lytle, 1996).

Subjective measures include: the emotions, motivations, and beliefs that parties to the negotiation develop, such as desire to interact in the future, trust in the other party, and so on (Lewicki & Polin, 2013).

2.12   Summary

There is remarkable agreement regarding the core concepts of negotiation across the disparate fields of economics, psychology, and labor–management negotiations. The central concepts of negotiation research provide a language and method by which researchers in different fields can collaborate and design research studies. The fundamental distinction between prescriptive and descriptive research divides the field of researchers into pure theorists and applied researchers. Many of these core concepts can be treated as independent (i.e., causal variables) or as dependent (i.e., effect) variables.

3 Behavioral decision making and negotiation

The behavioral decision-making approach had a profound impact on the empirical study of negotiation. The behavioral decision-making (BDM) approach was embraced by cognitive and social psychologists in psychology departments as well as management and organizational behavior scholars in business schools. This interdisciplinary mix created a hotbed of innovative research collaborations between economically trained management scientists and laboratory-based social psychologists. Fueled by the breakthrough research of Amos Tversky and Daniel Kahneman, two negotiation scholars, Max Bazerman and Margaret Neale pioneered the design and execution of voluminous research studies that combined the paradoxical insights of BDM with negotiation research.

3.1   Heuristics and Biases

The publication of Kahneman, Slovic, and Tversky's (1982) book, *Judgment Under Uncertainty: Heuristics and Biases* was a magnum opus that provided a blueprint for the design of behavioral research studies in negotiation. Tversky and Kahneman and their colleagues designed clever, simple "briefcase" experiments that essentially showed that people – even those who were highly motivated and intelligent – routinely and consistently violated the principles of rational decision making, as outlined by rational economic theory. Tverksy and Kahneman relied on economic theory, including von Neumann and Morgenstern's axioms to provide the "null hypothesis" for their experiments.

Tversky and Kahneman used the term "bias" to refer to systematic departures from a norm or standard. In other words, bias did not refer to random "noise" but rather consistent, predicable violations from

35

a norm or standard of rational behavior. What made their research so impactful was that behavioral and psychological science was suffering from a lack of perceived credibility. The critical thinking was, "if the results of a research study are obvious, then what was the point of doing the study (and funding social science research)"? Kahneman and Tversky found that people not only displayed paradoxical behavior, but their decisions led to sub-optimal outcomes, leading to economic loss and perhaps most notably, that most people regretted their decisions. This set the perfect stage for the research paradigm outlined by Raiffa – asymmetric, descriptive–prescriptive research. In other words, now that it has been shown that people engage in behaviors that are sub-optimal, how can researchers best help and re-educate the motivated decision maker? Behavioral scientists found that manager-students enrolled in business education programs were an ideal audience for these descriptive–prescriptive methods.

3.1.1   Risk and Uncertainty

The framing effect is perhaps the most well-known and well-researched of all of the documented decision-making biases. To understand the framing effect, it is important to understand the concept of risk and uncertainty from a prescriptive lens, as outlined by economists. According to economists, there are three main types of decisions: riskless choice (i.e., judgment under certainty), uncertainty, and risky choice.

3.1.1.1   Risky Decision Making

The theory of risky decision making is the study of gambles and "prospects" based on expected utility (EU) theory. EU theory dates back to the 16th century when French noblemen who played gambling games in their courts sought the advice and insight of mathematicians to inform their choices. Centuries later, von Neumann and Morgenstern (1944) developed the theory of rational behavior, based on the concept of a utility function. A utility function is a quantification of a person's preferences with respect to certain objects; assigning numbers to objects and to gambles that have objects as their prizes. von Neumann and Morgenstern postulated seven axioms of rational behavior, which if followed, would result in optimal (rational) choice when choosing among options.

3.1.1.1.1 Comparability Axiom

The comparability axiom is simple, but very important. It essentially states that everything is comparable on some dimension of "satisfaction." This essentially means that it is possible to compare eating a cheeseburger, losing one's luggage, or hugging one's child on a single dimension of satisfaction or utility. At first blush, that sounds harmless, but as we shall see, social scientists later found that people balk at making such comparisons (McGraw & Tetlock, 2005).

3.1.1.1.2 Closure Axiom

The closure axiom essentially states that it is possible to compare "gambles" to "sure things," such that if x and y are available alternatives, then so are all the gambles that involve chances of obtaining x and y. Decision making under risk is best expressed in the form of gambles that have specific payoff likelihoods.

3.1.1.1.3 Transitivity

The transitivity axiom is the most widely known axiom and it essentially states that people's preferences are assumed to be transitive, such that if a person prefers x to y, and y to z, then that person must therefore prefer x to z.

3.1.1.1.4 Reducibility

The reducibility axiom essentially states that a person's attitude toward a compound lottery is dependent only on the ultimate prizes and the chance of getting them, not on the actual gambling itself. This is a critical axiom because the theory of rational decision making only focuses on the expected utility of receiving the reward, and does not account for attitudes toward gambling itself.

3.1.1.1.5 Substitutability

The substitutability axiom states that gambles that have prizes about which people are indifferent are interchangeable.

3.1.1.1.6 Betweenness

The betweenness axiom states that if x is preferred to y, then x must be preferred to any probability mixture of x and y, which in turn must be preferred to y. Stated simply, if someone likes chocolate more than vanilla ice cream; then chocolate ice cream will be preferred to any gamble that involves a probability of getting chocolate or vanilla ice cream. And, such a gamble is consistently preferred over being served vanilla ice cream.

3.1.1.1.7 Continuity or Solvability

The continuity (or solvability) axiom states that if a person prefers $a>b>c$, then there must be a gamble involving a and c that is equivalent (in satisfaction) to a sure "b." Again, the axiom sounds simple enough, but suppose that a, b, and c are: getting a dime, getting a nickel, and being shot at dawn. This axiom states that there is a gamble involving receiving a dime and being shot at dawn is equally satisfying as receiving a nickel. Most people find this abhorrent (and wrong); however, economists argue that people have a very difficult time understanding extremely small probabilities.

3.1.1.2   Expected Utility

The expected utility principle (EU) was a key development in the study of individual decision making. As noted in Chapter 1, expected value (EV) was based on monetary value, the EU principle was based on utility (satisfaction). This may appear to be a trivial distinction, but it was quite profound. The important distinction between EV and EU can be understood by studying the St. Petersburg paradox (Bernoulli, 1954). In this simple demonstration, an unbiased coin is tossed until it lands on heads. The player of the game is paid \$2 if heads appears on the opening toss; \$4 if heads appears on the 2nd toss; \$8 if heads appears on the 3rd toss; \$16 if heads appears on the 4th toss, ad infinitum. The question for the rational decision maker (and rational choice theory) is how much should a risk-neutral player be willing to pay for the opportunity to play this game (guided only by the logic of rational decision making)?

This is where things get interesting. According to EV theory, a player should be willing to pay an infinite amount of money to play the game. Why? Because even though the likelihood of the coin landing on heads for any toss is 50%, there is a very small likelihood that the coin could, through random chance, land on tails for an infinite number of tosses. To be sure, the probability of this happening is infinitely small, but it is an infinitely small positive probability. Now, no one would be willing to pay an infinite amount of money to play – it seems absurd. But, this exactly where EV theory broke down and the theory of EU was developed.

According to EU theory, most people have a diminishing marginal utility for gains, such that the value of more and more money brings less and less pleasure (utility). Think of it this way: the difference between $0 and $100 seems vast; as compared to the difference between $100,000 and $100,100. However, because EV theory is based on a linear function of value, this sense of diminishing marginal utility was not captured. Conversely, EU theory is based not on the exact monetary value of gambles and prizes, but on how much "satisfaction" (utility) it brings, and utility functions therefore, do not have to follow strict linearity. For this reason, EU theory became known as "every man's utility function" (Bernoulli, 1954; Savage, 1954) following the principle of psychophysics, which states that good things satiate and bad things escalate (Coombs & Avrunin, 1977).

3.1.1.3   Prospect Theory

For a while, all seemed fine with EU theory. However, Kahneman and Tversky's (1979) prospect theory represented a major theoretical break-through and refinement for economics. Tversky and Kahneman refined EU theory by advancing a theory of subjectively expected utility. They did this by using Allais' paradox as a neat demonstration (Allais, 1953). The Allais paradox involves a choice problem that demonstrates the inconsist-ency of actual observed choices with the predictions of expected utility theory. Suppose you've been offered a choice between two different prizes, A and B. Prize A gives you a 50% chance of winning $3000; prize B offers you $1,000 for sure. Most people (typically over 80%) prefer the sure thing (i.e., prize B). Now, suppose that you've been offered a choice between a 5% chance of winning $3000 (prize C) and a 10% chance of $1000 (prize D). In this case, most people prefer to choose prize C. However, this choice violates the fundamental principle of choice because if we simply multiply prize A and B probabilities by 1/5 or 20%, this is mathematically identical to prize C and D, respectively. Thus, it is irrational for people to choose prize B over A; but then prize C over D.

Prospect theory introduced a probability-weighting function to reflect the idea that very small probabilities and very large probabilities are weighted differently; the difference between a 50% chance and a 55% chance does not seem as large as the difference between a 95% and a 100% chance.

Most astounding among Kahneman, Slovic, and Tversky's (1982) research findings was their demonstration of the framing effect (Tversky

& Kahneman, 1981; Levy, 1997). The framing effect states that people will be risk averse in the domain of gains, such that they will prefer a sure gain over a gamble with an equal or greater expected value; however, in the domain of losses, people will display risk-seeking behavior, choosing a gamble over a sure loss with an equal or lower expected loss.

3.2   Applications to Negotiation

Armed with the insights, clear, rational predictions of expected utility theory, and the empirical research pioneered by Kahneman and Tversky that showed striking and consistent departures from the theoretical predictions, Max Bazerman and Margaret Neale designed clever and compelling negotiation experiments revealing that negotiators engaged in sub-optimal behavior. Bazerman and Neale (1992) conceptualized negotiation as a straightforward two-party extension of individual decision making. They used the predictions of EU (expected utility) theory as a "null hypothesis" to test their hypotheses.

3.2.1   The Framing Effect

Bazerman and Neale designed experiments to examine prospect theory's framing effect in negotiation scenarios. The idea was that negotiators with a *gain* frame would be more likely to display risk aversion; but negotiators with a *loss* frame would display risk-seeking behavior. In a negotiation situation, the risk-averse approach is to accept proposals (that are better than one's reservation point and not risk a no-agreement alternative) conversely, the risk-seeking approach is to reject proposals and risk holding out for better terms where the likelihood of impasse increases. Thus, Neale and Bazerman expected that negotiators with a gain frame would be more concessionary (i.e., more likely to accept a proposal better than their reservation point) than negotiators with a loss frame.

In one of their first experiments, they used the induced-preference paradigm that assigned negotiators payoff schedules for a resource (Bazerman, Magliozzi, & Neale, 1985). The negotiation game contained a pareto-optimal (high joint gain) solution, but because the payoff schedules were private, this solution was not evident to negotiators. The major independent variable in their study was the payoffs themselves. For some of the negotiation pairs, the payoffs were presented as "monetary losses" (relative to a reference point); for other negotiation pairs, the payoffs were presented as "monetary gains" (relative to a reference point). Negotiators were then told to either "minimize their losses" (in the loss-frame condition) or maximize their gains (in the gain-frame condition).

According to Nash, any linear transformation of one's payoffs should not affect behavior or outcomes in negotiation. However, according to prospect theory, Bazerman and Neale predicted that negotiators who were facing losses (losing money) would behave in a more risk-seeking fashion; whereas negotiators who stood to make gains would be more risk averse. This is exactly what was found: negotiators who were assigned the "loss frame" were more likely to risk not reaching agreement at all (preferring to risk walking away from the table versus accepting a sure outcome); conversely, negotiators assigned to the "gain frame" were more likely to settle for outcomes (risk-averse behavior) rather than risk walking away from the table.

In several follow-up experiments, Bazerman and Neale and their colleagues further refined the framing effect in negotiation. They empirically documented that most negotiators are risk seeking when evaluating losses, but risk averse when evaluating gains. A *reference point* defines what a person considers to be a gain or a loss. In these investigations, negotiators who were instructed to "minimize their losses" made fewer concessions, reached fewer agreements, and perceived settlements to be less fair compared to those who were told to "maximize their gains" (Bazerman, Magliozzi, & Neale, 1985; Neale & Northcraft, 1986; Neale, Huber, & Northcraft, 1987; Neale & Bazerman, 1991). In short, the negotiators who were told to "minimize their losses" adopt more risky bargaining strategies preferring to hold out for a better, but more risky settlement. In contrast, those who are told to "maximize their gains" are more inclined to accept the sure thing.

3.2.2   Strategic Risk, BATNA Risk, and Contractual Risk

In negotiation, the concept of risk may apply to one of three aspects: strategic risk, such as the choice to use (or not use) certain tactics, BATNA risk (referring to how certain one's alternatives are) and contractual risk (referring to the likelihood that parties will indeed honor the terms of agreement).

When it comes to the use of strategies, negotiators often choose between extremely cooperative tactics (such as information sharing) and at the other extreme, competitive tactics (such as threats and demands). With regard to the risk of assessing one's outside alternatives, people's BATNAs may be uncertain because they are not guaranteed, but instead, may be likely.

Negotiators with a "gain frame" may be more risk averse (doubting the likelihood of their outside alternatives and therefore, more concessionary in a given negotiation) than negotiators with a "loss frame" (who might think their outside alternative is more likely than is actually the case).

One question concerns the implications of asymmetrically framed negotiators, such as if one negotiator has a negative frame and the other has a positive frame. The negotiator with the negative frame reaps a greater share of the resources (Bottom & Studt, 1993).

Another factor that affects behavior are the previous experiences a negotiator brings to the table. Negotiators who have recently experienced a string of failures are more likely to adopt a "loss frame" and feel less "in control" in a negotiation; conversely, negotiators who have experienced a recent string of successes feel greater control (Kray, Paddock, & Galinsky, 2008). Consequently, loss-framed negotiators are reluctant to reveal information that could be used to exploit them; instead, they prefer to manage risk by delaying outcomes.

Contractual risk refers to the risk associated with the willingness of the other party to honor its terms (Bottom, 1998). Negotiators with negative frames (risk seeking) are more likely to reach integrative agreements than those with positive frames (risk averse), because pursuing one's aspirations entails some creative risk. Thus, if integrative negotiation outcomes involve "sure things," positive frames are more effective; however, if the integrative outcomes require negotiators to "roll the dice," negative frames are more effective. In negotiations involving contractual risk, for example, negotiators with a "loss frame" are more cooperative and more likely to settle than those with a "gain frame" (Bottom, 1998). Further, "loss-frame" negotiators create more integrative agreements.

3.2.3   The Anchoring Effect

Anchoring is a decision bias first demonstrated by the work of Tversky and Kahneman. The anchoring bias occurs when a decision maker must make an estimate in the face of uncertainty and fails to make a sufficient adjustment from an arbitrary starting point. One of the most striking demonstration studies of the powerful anchoring effect was one in which people had to make estimates of the number of doctors in Manhattan (Wilson, Houston, Etling, & Brekke, 1996). To be sure, no one knows what that number is, so it is an example of decision making under uncertainty. The key finding was that people's estimates were strongly influenced by a random starting point. In their studies of negotiation, Neale and Bazerman (1991) reasoned that prior selling prices might act as anchors. The opening offers made by parties to a negotiation are very powerful anchors. Negotiators who make the first offer often have a strong distributive advantage in negotiation because their opening offer may anchor the counterparty. In this sense, a negotiator's first offer acts as an anchor for the counterparty's counteroffer.

As powerful as opening offers can be in anchoring the negotiation, many negotiators hesitate to make assertive opening offers because they worry that an extreme opening offer will "insult" the counterparty if they open too high (if they are selling) or too low (if they are buying). However, the fear of insulting the other party and souring the negotiations is more apparent than real. Indeed, people's perceptions of how assertive they can be with others are notably lower than what others actually believe (Ames, 2008).

Paradoxically, the anchoring strategy may come at the expense of subjective satisfaction with the deal. Buyers who use the anchoring tactic make higher profits (claim more value) than those who don't, but the counterparty believes their own outcome is worse than their expectations and consequently, they are less willing to interact in the future (Maaravi, Pazy, & Ganzach, 2014). In a market situation, anchoring decreases profit amongst negotiators because it increases the rate of impasse and prolongs negotiation.

3.2.4   Anchoring Information Model

Whereas the anchoring effect suggests making the opening offer is advantageous, the Anchoring Information Model (AIM) predicts when and why making the first offer is advisable (Loschelder, Trotschel, Swaab, Friese, & Galinsky, 2016). According to the AIM model, first offers have two effects: (1) they serve as anchors that pull final settlements toward the initial first offer value (anchoring), which usually produces a first-mover advantage; and (2) they convey information about the sender's priorities, which makes the sender vulnerable to exploitation and increases the risk of a first-mover disadvantage. Indeed, when senders did not reveal their priorities, they had a first offer advantage; however, when they revealed their priorities (either implicitly or explicitly), the first offer became a distinct disadvantage. This effect was strongest when the recipient of the offer was pro-self (versus pro-social).

Accordingly, negotiators need to consider two factors when making the first offer: how much information do they have regarding the negotiation and how much information does the other party have about them? A first-mover disadvantage exists in some situations where negotiators make first offers, particularly when there is significant *asymmetric* information (Loschelder, Trotschel, Swaab, Friese, & Galinsky, 2016).

In a situation in which the negotiator has good information and the other party is believed to also have good information, it is wise to make the first offer, so as to benefit from the anchoring effect. Indeed, when negotiators have good information, they are not likely to fall prey to the winner's curse (asking for too little) or the chilling effect (insulting the other party by making an outrageous offer). Instead, they can make an assertive opening offer that operates as a psychological anchor (Galinsky & Mussweiler, 2001). In the event that *both* parties lack information about the negotiated object or service in question, negotiators are advised to also make the opening offer. Given that *both* negotiators are ignorant about the market value of the object or item, the likelihood of insult is low and the anchoring effect may help the negotiator who is a first-mover.

In the case of significant, asymmetric information, the negotiator is best advised to not open first (Maaravi & Levy, 2017). This situation would be analogous to a "pawnshop" situation in which the negotiator is the pawnshop owner and has a lot of relevant knowledge and the counterparty is naïve and uninformed. In this situation, the negotiator does not run the risk of being "anchored" by the other party and there exists a possibility that the counterparty may fall victim to the winner's curse – either by not asking for enough or over-paying. Moreover, the pawnshop owner may be anchored by their own knowledge – so far better to prompt the naïve negotiator to open first. For these reasons, the negotiator should encourage the counterparty to make the opening offer.

The final situation to analyze is when the negotiator is naïve, but the counterparty has relevant information. This situation is analogous to a pawnshop negotiation wherein the focal negotiator is naïve and risks falling victim to the winner's curse by offering too much or asking for too little.

3.2.5   Over-Confidence

Over-confidence is a decision bias that is demonstrated when decision makers are asked to make an estimate under uncertainty and then attach confidence boundaries around that estimate. Kahneman and Tversky (1973) demonstrated the over-confidence effect in their studies when asking people to make estimates of unknown numbers (e.g., "what was the salary earned by the highest-paid CEO in a particular year?"; and "how many cubic feet of trash are…?"). Given that most people do not know the answers to such questions, they make estimates. The central dependent variable was measured by asking people to then put a confidence interval around their estimates such that they were 95% sure that the actual answer fell within that interval. The key finding was that people's confidence intervals were too narrow, suggesting they were over-confident about their estimates.

Bazerman and Neale (1982) cleverly demonstrated the over-confidence effect in their studies of negotiation and third-party intervention. Namely, they asked negotiators in a conflict situation to estimate the likelihood that a neutral third-party mediator would support their position. As it turns out, both parties to the conflict dramatically over-estimated the likelihood that a neutral third party would support their position. The implications were profound: when negotiators to conflict believe that neutral third parties will support them, they were less motivated to reach settlement and more likely to risk third-party arbitration or court action.

3.3   Fixed-Pie Perception

One of the most significant findings of Bazerman and Neale's prolific research program was a phenomenon that did not have roots in prospect theory – the fixed-pie perception. The fixed-pie perception is the (usually) faulty belief held by negotiators that the game is a fixed-sum situation, when in fact, it is a variable-sum situation. Stated differently, the fixed-pie perception is the belief that the other party's preferences are directly opposed to one's own interests.

When negotiators hold a fixed-pie perception, they focus primarily on "claiming" or the "distributive" aspect of negotiation. This can result in a regrettable state of affairs when they settle upon outcomes that are sub-optimal or pareto-inefficient.

Neale and Bazerman (1991) postulated the existence of a fixed-pie perception when they observed negotiators often engaging in compromise agreements, when in fact, a superior alternative was possible through a strategy known as logrolling. According to Froman and Cohen (1970) logrolling (a term borrowed from political science) occurs when negotiators make deep concessions on an issue of low-value in exchange for securing their most favorable terms on a highly valued issue. Logrolling can be empirically measured by using the "induced-preference" paradigm that assigns negotiator's utilities that can be assessed.

Whereas Bazerman and Neale postulated the existence of a fixed-pie perception, they had not measured it empirically. Thompson and Hastie (1990) developed a method to empirically document the existence of the fixed-pie perception. In a series of studies using the induced-preference paradigm, negotiators were asked (at several points in time) to make estimates of the counterparty's interests. By measuring their estimates, Thompson and Hastie found that the majority of negotiators (68%) believed the counterparty's interests were completely and diametrically opposed to their own (when in fact, this was not the case, as there existed an opportunity to reach a pareto-optimal solution by logrolling parties' interests). In one investigation, Thompson and Hastie measured fixed-pie perceptions several times during the negotiation (by interrupting parties and asking them for estimates). During the negotiation, fixed-pie perceptions diminished, and the negotiators who were able to abandon their early (faulty) fixed-pie perceptions ultimately settled for more profitable deals.

3.4   Summary

The JDM (judgment and decision-making approach) that characterized negotiation research for nearly two decades (1980s and 1990s) was distinctly cognitive. It focused on the negotiator as a "decision maker" and it assumed that the decision maker wanted to follow the norms and prescriptions of rational decision making (after all, who would willingly want to make choices that resulted in less utility [money] than other choices?). Fueled by the cognitive revolution, the constructs of relationships, emotion, and motivation were distinctly absent. It was after this era that researchers began to consider the distinctly social-psychological constructs of relationships, emotion, and motivation.

4 Relationships and social utility

The behavioral decision-making approach that was part of the cognitive revolution profoundly influenced negotiation research and theory in the 1980s and 1990s. Humans were viewed as cognitive information processors, cognitive misers, typically devoid of emotions and primarily intent upon maximizing economic utility. Expected Utility Theory and Prospect Theory provided the ideal standards that negotiators were held to, and empirical studies repeatedly found that negotiators came up short when held to the rational standard. A growing list of negotiator shortcomings and biases emerged, ranging from anchoring, to framing, to over-confidence. The behavioral literature paid relatively less attention to how negotiators might remedy, repair, or overcome biases.

4.1   Individual Rationality On Trial

However, not all researchers were enamored with the behavioral decision-making (BDM) approach that had been ushered in by behavioral economics. Moreover, the rational, information processing model of the negotiator seemed to be an unrealistic standard to hold people to; and it did not seem to characterize how real people often approached negotiation. Certainly, it was not the case that a dispassionate, intent-on-being rational person simply focused on their own outcomes with no regard for others.

For this reason, a group of social science researchers moved away from the narrow focus on gambles, choices, and utility functions, and began to examine the relational context of the negotiation. This body of research did not use EU or prospect theory as the standard by which negotiators were held to, but instead, examined how different social contexts, relationships, and motivations affected negotiation processes and outcomes. In addition to tossing aside the EU model as the "gold standard" of behavior, these researchers ushered back in a focus on the process of negotiation. Instead of a narrow focus on outcomes, researchers focused on the process of negotiation, including the content of communication, rationales, and subjective perceptions of the negotiators.

At the heart of the new focus on relationships in negotiation is the idea that successful negotiation is not simply focused on the maximization of monetary wealth, but instead, building and maintaining effective relationships. Making more money in a negotiation does not always lead to greater satisfaction (Thompson, 1995; Thompson, Valley, & Kramer, 1995; Galinsky, Mussweiler, & Medvec, 2002).

4.2   Subjective Value

At front and center of the relational view of negotiation was a new look at utility and satisfaction in negotiation. The BDM era had offered Prospect Theory – a refinement of the basic assumption of self-interest. Researchers in the "negotiation is a relationship" era questioned that very ideal, bluntly suggesting that the rational pursuit of self-interest, however tempered by a non-linear utility function, should not represent an ideal for the negotiator. Many of these researchers believed that negotiators wanted to maximize joint (not simply individual) welfare. Economists and behavioral researchers thought this idea was already represented in the subjective utility model – after all, negotiators could "care about" whatever brought them utility. However, that was not a satisfying response for many social science researchers who were not enamored with the economic model. These researchers were not influenced by the writings of economists and game theorists. Their backgrounds were steeped in social psychology.

4.2.1   Dual Concern Model

As noted in the opening chapter, one of the first theories to posit that negotiator utility (or satisfaction) should not be represented along a single continuum of satisfaction (or utility) was the Dual Concern Model (Pruitt & Carnevale, 1993). According to the Dual Concern Model, at any given time, negotiators had two concerns – one regarding the self and another concerning the other person. Because concern for the self was viewed as orthogonal to concern for the other, it was possible for negotiators to have any combination of concern for the self and the other party, including: high concern for the self/low concern for the other; low concern for the self/high concern for the other; low–low; and high–high. Integrative outcomes were only possible when negotiators had concern for the self and the other party, hence, dual concerns.

This theoretical model was tested by manipulating independent variables that would heighten concern for the self and separate independent variables that would heighten concern for the other. For example, in one investigation, Pruitt and his colleagues manipulated concern for the self by instructing negotiators that they were "accountable" to a constituency, who was presumably relying on the negotiator to bargain on their behalf (much like a lead union negotiator who has been elected to represent disgruntled constituents); concern for the other was separately manipulated by leading some negotiators to expect to interact with the counterparty in the near future on a cooperative task (Ben-Yoav & Pruitt, 1984a). Known as ECFI (expectation of cooperative future interaction), this expectation was believed to make the negotiator concerned about the other party. In his studies, Pruitt found that high self-concern, coupled with high concern for the other party, led to the most integrative outcomes.

There were criticisms of the Dual Concern Model. Demand characteristics might operate so that people assigned to the "concern about the other party" condition might feel compelled to meet the other party's interests. Other criticisms centered on the fact that instructing negotiators to try to maximize joint gains might in fact be a hint that the task was not zero-sum (Thompson & Hrebec, 1996).

4.2.2   Egocentric Bias

Years before the emergence of behavioral decision research, Messick and Sentis (1979) posited the existence of a *social utility* function, such that people's satisfaction with allocations of goods revealed that they cared not just about their own outcomes (as economists would argue), but also depended on the outcomes of others. Messick found evidence of an egocentric bias in social utility functions, such that people pay themselves substantially more than they are willing to pay others for doing the same task (Messick & Sentis, 1979). Specifically, people were asked: if they worked for 7 hours and were paid $25, while another person worked for 10 hours, how much did they think the other person should get paid? Most answered that the other person should get paid more for doing more work – about $30.29 on average. However, when asked how much should they get paid for 10 hours of work if the other person worked for 7 hours and got $25, the request was $35.24. The difference between $35.24 and $30.29 illustrates the phenomenon of egocentric bias.

4.2.3   Social Utility Function

Loewenstein, Thompson, and Bazerman (1989) examined people's preferences for several possible distributions of money for themselves and others. If people's utility functions were social (rather than individual), then their preferences would be affected by the other party's payoffs and not just by their own payoffs. Indeed, people's utility functions were social rather than individual, meaning that individual satisfaction was strongly influenced by both their own and the other party's payoffs. Social utility functions were tent-shaped: peaking when payoffs were the same for themselves and the other. Discrepancies between payoffs to the self versus the other led to lower satisfaction. However, social utility functions were lopsided in that advantageous inequity (when the self receives more than the other) was preferable to disadvantageous inequity (when the other receives more than the self). In addition, the nature of the relationship with the other party (e.g., positive, neutral, negative) affected satisfaction. In positive or neutral relationships, people preferred equity (for both gains and losses); in negative relationships, people preferred advantageous inequity. This meant that people rejected outcomes that entail one person receiving more than the other and opted for a settlement of lower joint value (pareto-inefficient), but equal-appearing shares (McClelland & Rohrbaugh, 1978).

4.2.4   Satisfaction versus Preference

In an intriguing follow-up study, Bazerman, White, and Loewenstein (1995) hypothesized that utility (i.e., negotiator satisfaction) and preference (i.e., choice) may not in fact be equivalent. Until this point, the research assumed that if people regarded one option as more appealing than another, then they would certainly choose that option if given the chance. Bazerman, Loewenstein, and White (1992) carefully constructed pairs of choices that involved a payoff to the self and a payoff to the "other." Some people were asked to choose between the payoffs and others were told to indicate their "satisfaction" (utility) with these outcomes. People's satisfaction and their actual choices did not follow the same preference ordering. Specifically, people were most likely to choose the option that gave them the greatest payoff, but at the same time, they regarded that option as less satisfying than another outcome.

4.2.5   Satisfaction and Performance

When satisfaction is decoupled from performance, this shakes the very foundations of economic theory. In one investigation, people negotiated and were given (false) feedback that the counterparty (opponent) either felt satisfied or not (Thompson, Valley, & Kramer, 1995). Negotiators' satisfaction was largely determined by how the other party reacted, and not by their own outcomes. In other words, if the other party appeared happy and satisfied, negotiators reasoned that they must have not done so well.

4.2.6   Subjective Value Inventory

Jared Curhan took the focus of social utility functions in negotiation one step further with his development of the subjective value inventory, or SVI (Curhan, Elfenbein, & Xu, 2006; Curhan, Elfenbein, & Kilduff, 2009). Moreover, Curhan further splintered negotiator utility (satisfaction), not just by focusing on the self and other, but by focusing on four concerns: (1) feelings about instrumental outcomes; (2) feelings about themselves; (3) feelings about the process; and (4) feelings about their relations with the people with whom they are negotiating. In an intriguing series of studies, Curhan found that SVI predicts MBA students' satisfaction with their employment compensation, job satisfaction, and reduced intentions to seek a different job a year later.

4.3   Relationships

Once the concept of negotiator utility was expanded to include subjective feelings about the other party, the lens widened to include the nature of the relationship. Just as negotiation researchers were convinced that people cared about the other party in a way that "payoff" schedules could not capture fully, they were also convinced that relationships mattered. It was one thing to instruct negotiators to anticipate future interaction with the counterparty; it was quite another thing to examine how friends, colleagues, or strangers might negotiate. Relationships influence not only the process of how people negotiate, it also influences their choice of with whom to negotiate (McGinn, 2006).

4.3.1   Studies of Real Relationships

Up until this point, most, if not all empirical research examined how strangers negotiate a fictitious item in a context that is distinctly short-term. A small body of research examined how people in long-term relationships negotiate. People rarely negotiate with complete strangers that they will never encounter again. Rather, people negotiate in long-term relationships with business partners, friends, and family. It would seem that negotiations with friends and trusted partners would present an ideal situation to reach integrative outcomes. When reaching mutual agreement is important, negotiators who have a relationship are more likely to discover integrative outcomes than those who do not have a relationship (Kray, Thompson, & Lind, 2005). Friends are more likely to adopt an expansive focus and create value-added tradeoffs that generate joint gains across negotiation contexts, not just merely within a given negotiation (McGinn & Keros, 2002).

In one of the earliest studies of relationships in negotiation, married couples were more cooperative than were ad hoc couples and reached agreements more quickly, but their outcomes were of lower joint value (Schoeninger & Wood, 1969). Similarly, Fry, Firestone and Williams (1983) examined negotiations among newlyweds and dating couples. Their performance was compared to a control group (complete strangers who shared no history). The "strangers" settled upon outcomes that were higher in joint value, however, the results were at marginally significant levels. The speculation was that couples were reluctant to set high targets and persist, and more inclined to settle for the first outcomes above their respective reservation points.

According to social scientists, the behavior of people in long-term relationships is guided by shared sets of rules (Argyle & Henderson, 1985; Clark & Mills, 1979). Relationships influence not only the process of how people negotiate but also their choice of an interaction partner (McGinn,

2006). For example, negotiators who reach an impasse find themselves getting caught in "distributive spirals" in which they interpret their performance as unsuccessful, experience negative emotions, and develop negative perceptions of their negotiation counterparts and the entire negotiation process (O'Connor, Arnold, & Burris, 2005). Moreover, negotiators who reach an impasse in a prior negotiation are more likely to do the same in their next negotiation or to reach low-value (lose–lose) deals compared to negotiators who were successful in reaching agreement (O'Connor, Arnold, & Burris, 2005). Moreover, this effect holds true even when the negotiator is dealing with a different person.

Several research investigations have examined how people negotiate with friends in long-term relationships. People expect more generous negotiation offers from close others (Ramirez-Fernandez, Ramirez-Marin, & Munduate, 2018). Moreover, when their expectations are not met, negative emotions arise that can harm the quality of negotiated agreements. However, to the extent that negotiators in close relationships engage in perspective-taking, they can monitor their expectations and reach successful outcomes (Ramirez-Fernandez, Ramirez-Marin, & Munduate, 2018).

At first blush, it would seem that negotiating with friends and loved ones would present an ideal situation to reach pareto-optimal outcomes. Levels of cooperative behavior decrease as social distance increases between people (Buchan, Croson, & Dawes, 2002). Friends who find themselves at the bargaining table are more likely to adopt an expansive focus and create value-added tradeoffs that generate joint gains across negotiation contexts, not just merely within a given negotiation (Valley, Neale, & Mannix, 1995). McGinn and Keros (2002) examined negotiations among strangers and friends and found that one of three patterns emerges early on, including: opening up (complete and mutual honesty) working together (cooperative problem-solving); and haggling (competitive deal-making). Conversely, when strangers interact, they often begin in haggling mode. In contrast, friends begin to open up almost immediately.

However, negotiating with friends and loved ones may actually at times make it more difficult to reach pareto-optimal outcomes. Friends are less competitive with each other than they are with strangers (Valley, Neale, & Mannix, 1995). Friends exchange more information, offer greater concessions, fewer demands, and are more generous with one another (Mandel,

2006). Consequently, negotiators in a relationship are often unable to profitably exploit opportunities to create value.

4.3.2   Unmitigated Communion

Unmitigated communion refers to the fact that people believe they should be responsive to others' needs and not assert their own (Amanatullah, Morris, & Curhan, 2008). Because people often feel uncomfortable negotiating with friends (Kurtzberg & Medvec, 1999), they may make relational sacrifices. Relational accommodation occurs when people make economic sacrifices to preserve relationships. For example, friends are less competitive at the negotiation table than strangers (Valley, Neale, & Mannix, 1995). Friendship dictates that we should be concerned with fairness and the other person's welfare, while negotiations dictate that we should get a good deal for ourselves (Kurtzberg & Medvec, 1999). These two dictates are in conflict with one another. Relational accommodation occurs when people make economic sacrifices to preserve relationships. Most friendships are built on communal norms, which mandate that we should take care of people we love, respond to their needs, and not "keep track" of who has put in what (Clark & Mills, 1979). Thus, the communal norm prescribes that we should be sensitive to the needs of people we love or like and attempt to meet those needs, rather than try to maximize our own interests. The opposite of communal norms are exchange norms, which state that people should keep track of who has invested in a relationship and be compensated based on their inputs.

4.3.3   Relational Construal

People in a relationship might share very different views about that relationship. Relational Self-Construal (RSC) refers to how people view their relationship, on a continuum of high relationship to low relational focus (Gelfand, Smith Major, Raver, Nishii, & O'Brien, 2006). When both negotiators have a high relationship focus, there is a tendency to satisfice, or make economic sacrifices to preserve the relationship. When one negotiator has a high relationship focus and the other has a low relationship focus, there is distancing, whereby parties to the relationship do not focus on building the relationship; when both are low in relationship focus, economic concerns become the shared focus and parties can engage in trading and transaction. According to the model, integrative outcomes are more likely when negotiators are moderately focused on the relationship.

4.3.4   Long-term Negotiations

One criticism leveled at negotiation research is the short-term focus. In reality, negotiations often take place in the context of long-term relationships. The new focus on relationships also focused on how previous negotiations affected future ones. For example, negotiators who fail to reach agreement in a prior negotiation are more likely to get caught in a "distributive spiral" in which they interpret their performance as unsuccessful, experience negative emotion, and develop negative perceptions of the counterparty (O'Connor, Arnold, & Burris, 2005). This carry-over effect is so powerful, it even influences people who interact with a new negotiation partner.

4.3.5   Reactive Devaluation

Economic theory predicts that people's satisfaction with outcomes should only depend on the nature of the outcome (prize) itself; and not on the mechanism or source. The phenomenon of reactive devaluation illustrates that people's satisfaction is affected by the source of the proposal. Oskamp (1965) found that people tended to devalue and distrust proposals as a function of who offered them (rather than their actual content). In Oskamp's study, Americans were presented with 50 different proposals about how to end the Cold War that were either allegedly put forth by U.S. or Russian diplomats (Oskamp & Hartry, 1968). In actual fact, it was completely random as to who the alleged author was. Nevertheless, there was a strong devalue-the-author effect: 320 people considered 50 proposals concerning the Cold War and the only difference was whether the proposal was allegedly authored by the U.S. or Russia. On nearly every proposal – 46 out of 50 – attitudes were driven by the alleged author of the proposal – not the content of the proposal itself. Moreover, differences ranged as high as 4 points on a 6 point "likeability" scale!

Years later, Ross and Stillinger (1991) examined people's utility (satisfaction) regarding proposed solutions in a conflict situation. The conflict involved the traditionalist educators in disagreement with revisionist educators in California school systems and concerned which books should form the core of the English curriculum. Not surprisingly, the traditionalists preferred the "classics" – for example, *Macbeth*, *The Iliad*, *Paradise Lost*, and so on. The revisionists preferred a different set of books that would involve more diverse viewpoints, including *Mrs. Dalloway*, *The Woman Warrior*, *Native Son*, and so on. Each of the groups (i.e., traditionalists and revisionists) were asked to *predict* what books the opposing party would want on the school curriculum (Robinson & Keltner, 1996; Ross & Stillinger, 1991; Stillinger, 1988). The opposing camps assumed that they would have *no* choices in common, when in actual fact, both parties shared seven books in common, dramatically more than they realized! When negotiators dismiss suggestions offered by the opposing side (e.g., "If they want it, then it can't be good for us"), this is known as reactive devaluation (Ross & Stillinger, 1988).

4.4   Reputation

People who interact in social and professional networks quickly develop reputations. The more central a role or position one holds in a network, the more likely it is that reputations will quickly form (Anderson & Shirako, 2008). Reputations in negotiation are built on first-hand experience and second-hand information, such that a person might develop a reputation even though they have not personally interacted with others. Reputations are highly evaluative, meaning that they are either "good" or "bad." Reputations affect how counterparties interact in negotiations (Glick & Croson, 2001). Glick and Croson (2001) investigated the emergence of four types of reputations that emerged in a negotiation community: "liar-manipulator" (will do anything to gain advantage), "tough, but honest" (makes very few concessions, but will not lie), "nice and reasonable" (makes concessions) and "cream puff" (makes concessions and is conciliatory regardless of what the other party does). Not surprisingly, people act much tougher when dealing with someone who has the reputation for being a liar (61% reported using distributive tactics with these people). Against tough negotiators, competitive behavior dropped to 49% and integrative strategies were used 35% of the time. Those facing "nice" negotiators used distributive tactics 30% of the time and 64% integrative tactics, but when facing a "cream puff," 40% used distributive tactics and only 27% used integrative tactics.

It is not just the type of negotiator that affects reputations, even a person known to have negotiation experience can create a reputation that leads counterparties to behave more defensively. Novice negotiators who interacted with "expert" negotiators who had distributive reputations evaluated their counterpart more negatively and used more distributive

and less integrative strategies, ultimately leading to less integrative outcomes (Tinsley, O'Connor, & Sullivan, 2002). When the novices were told
that the expert had an integrative reputation, the novices disclosed more
information which resulted in higher joint gains.

4.5   Situational Cues

Just as researchers were intent on focusing on how relationships affected
the process and outcome of negotiation, they also focused on the
context, reasoning that a business negotiation might very well differ from
a personal negotiation. Loewenstein, Thompson, and Bazerman (1989)
explored business version personal negotiation and found differences
in the social utility function, such that people were more likely to prefer
equality when negotiating in a personal situation, rather than a business
situation.

Ross and his colleagues used the PDG game (prisoner's dilemma game)
to examine behavior (Liberman, Samuels, & Ross, 2004). Some people
played the "Wall Street game"; others played the "community game." In
all situations, the payoffs were identical, but the name-of-the-game profoundly affected behavior with people making more competitive choices
in the Wall Street game than in the community game, despite identical
payoffs.

4.6   Summary

The focus on relationships in negotiation marked a renaissance period
for behavioral negotiation research. The research investigations in this
new era developed new methods and paradigms that expanded not only
the causal factors that might affect negotiation outcomes, including the
nature of parties' relationship, their relationship motivations, and the
context of the negotiation itself, it also expanded the outcomes of negotiation to include: satisfaction, willingness to interact in the future, and
trust in the other party.

5   Emotion revolution

The new focus on relationships and social utility appealed to researchers who were keen to use theories of social relationships to enrich and broaden the study of negotiation. Simply focusing on the economic aspects of negotiation, to the exclusion of personality, emotion, motivation, communication, and relationships seemed incomplete. The focus on relationships and social utility raised new questions about the emotional and motivational state of the negotiator. Previous decades had been shaped by the cognitive revolution that likened the decision maker (and negotiator) to a computer who processed information and optimized choices, all the while maintaining composure. This view of the negotiator as a cool-headed information processor, did not sit well with social psychologists who had studied the work of Hans Eysenck (1982), Richard Lazarus (1991), and other researchers who posited that emotion affected human behavior. A large research tradition in social psychology put the role of emotion as front-and-center stage, arguing that hot cognition (emotion) drove behavior (Zajonc, 1980). Even the theory of cognitive dissonance posited that hot emotional states (the discomfort felt from being incongruent) spurred behavioral and cognitive change (Zajonc, 1968).

5.1   From Cold to Hot Information Processing

Following the "cognitive revolution" fueled by the BDM (behavioral decision making) era with Prospect Theory as its calling card, the "emotion revolution" emerged in negotiation research, guided by researchers in social psychology as well as management fields. These researchers ushered the emotional life of the negotiator back into their theories and constructs focusing on how emotion, including mood, affects the course and outcome of negotiation. Thus, negotiation research started to become "hot" instead of coolly rational.

5.2   Dual Routes

One of the key distinctions that legitimized the social actor as an "emotional" decision maker is the dual-information processing model. According to the dual-information processing model, some information is thoughtfully and deliberately weighted and evaluated (central route); whereas other information is not consciously evaluated and weighted but nevertheless affects behavior (peripheral route). Evans (2008), Kahneman (2011), and Fiske and Taylor (2017) noted that the central and peripheral route were distinctly different. The central route was used in a deliberate, thoughtful, and conscious fashion; whereas the peripheral route often operated without conscious awareness, using hunches, and intuition – that the perceiver did not necessarily have access to. Years later, Kahneman's book, *Thinking Fast and Slow* (2011) articulated similar, dual routes for processing information and making decisions. The two routes, posited researchers, may also influence negotiation behavior.

5.3   Emotion and Mood

Emotion is not the same as mood. Emotions are typically fleeting states, that are usually fairly intense and often a result of a particular event. Conversely, moods are more chronic, longer in duration, and more diffuse, meaning that moods are usually not the result of or directed at a particular person or event; moods are often longer in duration. Emotions are complex and span the gamut from anger, regret, relief, gratitude, joy and so on. Conversely, moods are typically described as either positive or negative. The PANAS scale (positive and negative affect scale), can reliably measure mood states (Watson, Clark, & Tellegen, 1988). Moreover, researchers experimented with inducing mood states to examine the impact of positive and negative affect on behavior, decision making, and negotiation. The induction of mood states usually involves asking a negotiator to think about a time they were especially positive and content (or conversely negative and upset) and to describe that time in as much detail as possible.

5.3.1 Mood as a Temporarily Activated State

One of the first studies of mood and its impact on negotiation was a simple demonstration study in which one party used humor, presumably creating a good mood (O'Quinn & Aronoff, 1981). Alice Isen and her colleagues pioneered the study of positive affect on a number of social interactions, including problem-solving (Isen, 2001; 2002a), decision making (Isen, 2001; Isen & Labroo, 2003), persuasion, and negotiation, and their work was instrumental for understanding how mood affects behavior (Isen, 2000; 2002b; 2004). Isen used her theory of positive affect and creativity (Isen, 1999) to derive the prediction that good mood should lead to more creative thinking, a key skill thought to be associated with reaching integrative outcomes in negotiation (Isen, Daubman, & Nowicki, 1987). In one investigation, Carnevale and Isen (1986) examined how mood affected negotiation outcomes. They manipulated mood as an independent variable and in the "good mood" condition, they arranged for study participants to unexpectedly find a dime in a phone booth. In a subsequent negotiation situation, the study participants who had found the dime created more integrative (high joint value) outcomes than did those in the neutral (did not find the dime) condition. Subsequent research investigations manipulated mood using different methods, including watching comedic films and found the same effect: in general, participants in a good mood were more likely to create integrative (high joint value) deals in negotiation.

Kopelman, Rosette, and Thompson (2006) examined how three types of mood displays by negotiators (positive, neutral, negative) affected outcomes. In this study, they manipulated not how the focal negotiator felt, but instead, the question was how negotiators would react when confronted with a positive, neutral, or negative opponent. In this situation, participants were told they were negotiating fees for a wedding service and there was a dispute about the charges on the bill. They saw a film clip then of the opponent who either was positive, neutral, or negative and the key dependent variable was how would the negotiator respond to these displays. The key findings were that negotiators were more responsive to the use of positive and neutral affect than negative affect.

5.3.2   Mood as a Chronic State

Other research investigations did not attempt to manipulate mood through techniques such as finding dimes or watching films, but instead conceptualized mood as a chronic state that could be measured reliably with instruments. One of the key instruments used to measure chronic mood is the PANAS (Positive and Negative Affect Schedule) (Watson, Clark, & Tellegen, 1988). Anderson and Thompson (2004) used the PANAS to study how chronic mood affects negotiation. They tested the hypothesis that the positive affect of powerful negotiators shapes the quality of negotiation processes and outcomes more than the positive affect of less powerful negotiators. The findings from two studies supported the hypothesis: powerful individuals' trait positive affect was the best predictor of negotiators' trust for each other and of whether they reached integrative outcomes. Positive affect predicted joint gains above and beyond negotiators' trait cooperativeness and communicativeness. However, positive affect was unrelated to distributive outcomes; thus, there were no observed disadvantages of being positively affective.

5.4   Emotion in Negotiation

Emotion in negotiation can be studied as an independent (causal) variable; or as a dependent (effect variable). Stated differently, emotions can cause certain behaviors and outcomes to emerge in negotiation. Similarly, certain negotiation behaviors might lead negotiators to feel certain emotions. Much research has focused on the first type, namely emotion as a causal variable.

5.4.1   Anger

Anger is a common emotion in conflict and negotiation. Anger is an emotion that is most often reciprocated, meaning that anger expressed by person A leads to an expression of anger by person B (Friedman, Anderson, Brett, Olekalns, Goates, & Lisco, 2004; Parkinson, 1996). Reciprocation of anger escalates conflict and can prevent negotiators from reaching agreement and hinder the development of integrative outcomes. Negotiators who are angry and feel little compassion for the counterparty are less effective in terms of reaching integrative agreements than are happy negotiators (Allred, Mallozzi, Matsui, & Faia, 1997).

However, not all negative emotions have the same consequences or activate the same regions of the brain (Olekalns & Druckman, 2014). Unlike anger, disappointment is not a reciprocal emotion. Rather, disappointment often generates a complementary response such that when person A expresses disappointment, person B wants to repair the disappointment. It may seem that expressing disappointment would signal weakness; on the other hand, it may invite the other party to help. Indeed, one investigation examined how people responded to an opponent who was disappointed or worried versus an unemotional opponent. People conceded more when the opponent was disappointed and conceded the least when the opponent showed guilt (van Kleef, DeDreu, & Manstead, 2006). Expressing disappointment is particularly effective with people who are highly self-interested. Indeed, people who are self-interested see disappointment as a threat to getting what they want (van Kleef & Van Lange, 2008).

5.4.2   EASI Model

According to the Emotion as Social Information (EASI) model, displays of anger can lead to concessions by the counterparty, but only under certain conditions (van Kleef, Anastasopoulou, & Nijstad, 2010). Ultimately, the effect of anger displays depends upon several factors, including the counterparty's expectation that low offers will be rejected; the negative consequences of rejecting the angry negotiator's offer, the counterparty's reservation price, and the perceived authenticity of the anger emotion (Adam & Brett, 2015).

5.4.3   Genuine versus Strategic Emotion

In a negotiation situation, people may use emotion to strategically manipulate or persuade the counterparty. And so, negotiators often question whether emotions and moods are in fact, genuine or strategic. One investigation examined "surface-acting anger" (e.g., showing anger that is not genuinely felt, but instead displayed for strategic reasons) and "deep-acting anger" (e.g., expressing anger that is truly experienced; Cole, Hideg, & van Kleef, 2013). As compared to deep-acting anger, surface-acting anger backfired, leading to increased demands and reduced trust by the receiving party. Another investigation examined happy versus angry negotiators who were either perceived as authentic or inauthentic and found that counterparties concede more to authentically angry counterparties (Tng & Au, 2014).

The ability to detect strategic emotion would seem to be an advantage for negotiators. People who are low in dialectical thinking are more likely to believe that counterparties might use negative emotion for personal gain and react negatively (Hideg & van Kleef, 2017).

5.5   Empathy and Perspective-Taking

Empathy is an emotional skill in which the negotiator attempts to feel what the other person is feeling. Most social science suggests that the ability to feel empathy has positive consequences for behavior, including negotiation. Indeed, people are hardwired to be empathic with those closest to them because when we're close with someone, they become part of ourselves (Beckes, Coan, & Hasselmo, 2012).

Adam Galinsky and his colleagues examined the impact of empathy on negotiation (Galinsky, Maddux, Gilin, & White, 2008). Galinsky reasoned that negotiators who are instructed to be empathic may not as effective in discovering the counterparty's interest and constructing integrative (i.e., AEI solutions) as negotiators who engaged in perspective-taking. Whereas it might seem that empathy and perspective-taking are the same thing, there is a subtle and important difference. Empathy focuses people on how the other party is feeling; conversely, perspective-taking focuses people on how the other party is thinking. Galinsky and colleagues hypothesized that negotiators who engaged in perspective-taking would be more likely to reach integrative outcomes than negotiators who engaged in empathy and that is what they found (Galinsky, Maddux, Gilin, & White, 2008; Gilin, Maddux, Carpenter, & Galinsky, 2013).

Perspective-taking is a technique in which people try to imagine how the other person thinks. When people *think* about the other person's point of view, they are more effective in finding integrative outcomes than when they simply try to *feel* what the other person is feeling. Thus, perspective-taking is different from pure empathy. Whereas perspective-taking is a *cognitive* ability to consider the world from another's viewpoint, empathy is the ability to emotionally connect with another person (Galinsky, Maddux, Gilin, & White, 2008). To be sure, perspective-taking and empathy are both useful in different types of negotiations: Perspective-taking leads to more accurate understanding of other parties in negotiation, whereas empathy produces greater emotional understanding (Gilin, Maddux, Carpenter, & Galinsky, 2013). Negotiators who either are high in perspective-taking ability or are prompted to take the perspective of the counterparty are more successful in identifying and reaching integrative outcomes in negotiation.

5.6   Trust, Distrust, and Suspicion

Trust is a person's willingness to make themselves vulnerable to another (Rousseau, Sitkin, Burt, & Camerer, 1998). There are several types of trust, including: benevolence-based trust, deterrence-based trust, and empathy-based trust (Shapiro, Sheppard, & Cheraskin, 1992; Lewicki & Bunker, 1996), which has not been empirically studied in negotiation as much as what might be believed, judging how much concern lay people put in trust. The most straightforward research prediction is that trust would be positively related to negotiation outcomes. However, the research suggests that the relationship between trust and negotiation performance may be more complex.

One research investigation tested the impact of trust, distrust, and suspicion on negotiated outcomes (Sinaceur, 2010). They hypothesized that trust may not be as effective in helping negotiators reach integrative outcomes as would suspicion. The hypothesis was that when people distrust someone, they have negative expectations about their motives. However, when they are suspicious, they are uncertain of another's motives. Distrust leads to withdrawal (or combat), but suspicion can lead to questioning. When a negotiator is suspicious of their opponent, they are more likely to reach more integrative agreements than when they are not suspicious (Sinaceur, 2010).

5.7   Motivation

Just as emotion is considered to be a "hot" state; so is motivation. Whereas early research focused on three motivational goals, individualistic, competitive, and cooperative, later research focused on motivation as an approach-avoidance goal, involving promotion and prevention.

5.8   Prevention and Promotion

Higgins' (1998; 2005) theory of promotion and prevention as key goal states had a profound influence on social psychology, further cementing the move away from cool information processing that had dominated during the previous decades. According to Higgins (1998; 2005) people's orientation toward others and events could either be one of approach (promotion goal) or avoidance (prevention goal). At first blush, it would appear that promotion–prevention is an extension (or reformulation) of Prospect Theory. However, that is not the case. Prospect theory was a "cool" theory in that the decision maker was presumed to be guided by the desire to be rational and that reference points defined "gains" and "losses." Conversely, promotion–prevention theory was a "hot" theory in that the social actor was either in a goal-seeking state or an avoidance-state.

Promotion-focused negotiators conceptualize goals as ideals and opportunities; conversely *prevention-focused* negotiators conceptualize goals as obligations and necessities. Promotion-focused negotiators who focus on "ideals" rather than "oughts" do better in terms of claiming value (Galinsky & Mussweiler, 2001). Indeed, negotiators who focus on their ideals and aspirations claim more resources than those who focus on avoiding negative outcomes, holding constant their actual economic positions (Galinsky, Leonardelli, Okhuysen, & Mussweiler, 2005). However, the ultimate success of promotion- and prevention-focused negotiations hinges upon the aggressiveness of their targets (aspirations). Prevention-focused negotiators who set goals in the upper end of the ZOPA are less likely to concede and outperform promotion-focused negotiators (Trotschel, Bundgrens, Huffmeier, & Loschelder, 2013).

Promotion and prevention focus affect subjective outcomes as well. Negotiators who focus on ideals do not feel as satisfied as negotiators who focus on their reservation point or BATNA (Thompson, 1995). This is known as the *goal-setting paradox* (Freshman & Guthrie, 2009). Thus, focusing on an ideal target will lead to an attractive outcome, but it may not feel satisfying. In contrast, focusing on reservation points leads people to *do* worse but *feel* better. If negotiators think about their BATNA after the negotiation, they feel better (Galinsky, Mussweiler, & Medvec, 2002).

In price negotiations, buyers and prevention-focused people prefer *vigilant* strategies, whereas sellers and promotion-focused people prefer *eager* strategies (Appelt & Higgins, 2010). When there is a match between a negotiator's role (buyer, seller) and their strategy, the negotiator is more demanding in the situation.

5.9   Mindset

Another psychological factor that influences negotiation is mindset. Rooted in attribution theory, the idea is that people differ with respect to their control over certain behaviors. People with an internal locus of control believe they can change their behaviors; people with an external locus of control believe that situational factors are responsible. Kray and her colleagues demonstrated how nurture can triumph over nature in an intriguing investigation. Kray led people to believe that being successful in negotiation was either due to genetic gifts (i.e., nature) or hard work and effort (i.e., nurture) (Kray & Haselhuhn, 2008). The *naturists* have *fixed mindsets* – you either have it or you don't. Conversely, nurturists have *growth* mindsets – they believe you can develop skills. Kray's results pointed to a self-fulfilling prophesy. When people adopted a fixed mindset, they were *less likely* to reach integrative outcomes; conversely, when they adopted a growth mindset and viewed negotiation as a challenge, they were more successful in reaching high-quality deals (O'Connor, Arnold, & Maurizio, 2010). People who believe that negotiation ability can be improved with experience and practice are more likely to discover integrative agreements than people who believe that negotiation skills are not teachable (Wong, Haselhaun, & Kray, 2012).

One reason why negotiation skills training can be challenging is that people believe it will require a lot of effort and deplete their mental reserves. This is why people often want an "easy" solution to a problem. Case in point: One investigation introduced negotiation strategies to learners framed as either "easy" versus "difficult." In actuality, the strategies were exactly the same! The negotiators who were told the strategies were "easy" were more likely to successfully adopt the strategy and achieve integrative outcomes than when the same strategy was framed as "difficult" (Giacomantonio, Ten Velden, & DeDreu, 2016).

5.10   Summary

The emotion revolution that characterized negotiation research introduced a broad array of new independent variables that formed the basis of new theories. The emotion revolution moved away from the economic models that defined rationality and the research questions no longer focused on the ways in which people departed from rational models. Instead, the focus was on how do different types and intensities of emotion affect the bargaining process and outcome? Several of these investigations tested innovative (and counterintuitive) hypotheses. The researchers of this area embraced the hot cognition that had been part of the history of social psychology and found new and creative ways to examine emotion and mood in negotiation. These researchers primarily relied on manipulating, however temporarily, mood states and emotions.

6 Gender

A gender[1] pay gap between men and women has persisted over time – in a 2019 analysis, a United States Census Bureau report found that women in the United States earned 82% of what men earned (Semega, Kollar, Shrider, & Creamer, 2020; Barroso & Brown, 2021). While gender differences in human capital (e.g., level of schooling and work experience) partially explain why a pay gap exists, it cannot fully explain the pay gap (Blau & Kahn, 2017). As a result, researchers have considered the role of gender in negotiations for why these disparities have emerged.

Similar to the research examining the effects of individual differences on negotiations (see Chapter 7), research on the effects of gender on negotiation processes and outcomes has gone through several evolutions over the past several decades. In the 1970s and early 1980s, a central area of examination was the effect of gender on negotiations. Yet, the empirical research often produced a lack of conclusive evidence of reliable effects of gender on negotiation outcomes (see Rubin & Brown, 1975; Thompson, 1990, for reviews). For example, Rubin and Brown (1975) found that, across 68 experiments, in approximately one-third of the studies, men used more cooperative negotiation tactics than women; in another third of the studies, women used more cooperative tactics than men; and in the final third of studies, no gender differences emerged. As a result of this lack of conclusion, this area of work did not receive much attention for several decades.

Around the turn of the century, the examination of gender began to regain traction. Three streams of interest emerged around understanding gender differences: in the propensity to negotiate, in economic outcomes, and in non-economic outcomes. Moreover, the new research conducted highlighted the importance of examining key negotiator and situational moderators.

6.1   The Propensity to Negotiate

A large area of research has examined gender differences in the likelihood to negotiate, with the finding that men tend to exhibit a higher propensity to negotiate than women. One reason for this is that women may be more structurally disadvantaged than men. For example, in a recent article, Sauer, Valet, Shams, and Tomaskovic-Devey (2021) examined 2,400 German employees and found that women were less likely to possess the opportunity to negotiate than men – in other words, they were likely to be in jobs in which negotiations were not possible. Moreover, the authors found that even when given the opportunity, women still were less likely to initiate negotiation than men.

This gender difference in initiating negotiation was highlighted in the seminal book on gender and negotiations titled *Women Don't Ask*

The rationale for this gender difference draws from social role congruity theory, which suggests that people will be more positively evaluated when they are perceived to possess traits and characteristics that are congruent with their gender role (Eagly & Karau, 2002). Social role congruity theory suggests that women will perform worse than men in negotiation because of the incongruence between their gender and negotiation role. For example, women are expected to be less assertive and agentic, a trait often associated with negotiation success. As a result, the role incongruity that emerges when women negotiate may both influence both women's self-perceptions and external perceptions. Drawing from this theorizing, below we outline two areas of research examining the reasons behind gender differences in negotiation initiation. The first reason is that, as compared to men, women tend to harbor greater negative emotions and perceptions toward negotiations. A second related reason is that, as compared to men, women face greater backlash for negotiating.

6.1.1   Women's Self-Perceptions and Negotiation Perceptions

Individuals face stereotype threat (anxiety and concern) when the negative stereotypes related to their social group are made salient. In terms of negotiations, women tend to experience greater stereotype threat than men because of role incongruity between their gender role and the negotiation task (Kray, Thompson, & Galinsky, 2001). As a result, women are less likely to initiate negotiations than men because they experience greater anxiety and apprehension about negotiating (Babcock, Gelfand, Small, & Stayn, 2006; Small, Gelfand, Babcock, & Gettman, 2007). Moreover, even if they do take part in a negotiation, women feel more relieved than men when their first offer is accepted (Kray & Gelfand, 2009). Finally, researchers have found that women feel less efficacious about their negotiation ability than men (Stevens, Bavetta, & Gist, 1993) and are less likely to see situations as negotiable.

6.1.2   Backlash

Because women are less likely to initiate negotiations than men, one belief is that women should always attempt to negotiate more (Exley, Niederle, & Vesterlund, 2020).

However, an important reason to temper this belief is that women receive more backlash than men for negotiating because doing so is seen as stereotype-incongruent behavior (Bowles, Babcock, & Lai, 2007). In one set of studies, women were perceived as less likeable when they acted assertively in negotiations (Amanatullah & Tinsley, 2013). Moreover, in another set of studies by Bowles, Babcock, and Lai (2007), evaluators were less willing to work with women candidates who attempted to negotiate higher compensation in a job negotiation; however, this effect did not emerge for male candidates. Moreover, this effect was more prominent when the evaluators were male (versus female). The women were per-ceived to be less nice and more demanding when they initiated negotia-tions as compared to when they didn't.

Because of the potential for backlash, women may be more strategic in their decisions to enter negotiations. This possibility was tested in a study by Exley, Neiderle, and Vesterlund (2020). In this study, women and men took part in a simulated negotiation between "workers" and "firms." The "workers" received an initial offer to work at the firm and then were either assigned to a condition in which they chose whether or not to negotiate or a condition in which they were forced to negotiate. The researchers found that women who were forced to negotiate did not financially benefit from negotiating – in fact, results suggested that the negotiations even harmed their final compensation levels (potentially due to backlash). In contrast, women gained more financially when they had the choice to negotiate. This was because women in the choice condition were more likely to enter into negotiations that financially benefitted them and to avoid negotiations which would be financially harmful. Men, on the other hand, seemed less adept at knowing when to initiate negotiations, and were more likely to enter them regardless of whether the outcomes financially harmed or helped them. These results suggest that women will only enter into negotiations when it has the potential to benefit them in terms of final compensation.

6.1.3   Negotiation Context Moderators

While Kugler, Reif, Kaschner, and Brodbeck (2018) found a gender difference in negotiation initiation, their meta-analysis also demonstrated that the effect depended on characteristics of the social context. Specifically, there is evidence that the situational ambiguity and salient gender role cues can help overcome women's reduced willingness to negotiate.

6.1.3.1   *Situational Ambiguity*

Situational ambiguity refers to "the degree of uncertainty in parties' understanding of the economic structure of the negotiation" (Bowles, Babcock, & McGinn, 2005, p. 952). Kugler, Reif, Kaschner, and Brodbeck (2018) found that when situational ambiguity is low (i.e., it is clear in the situation that negotiating is acceptable), both men and women perceived that negotiating is acceptable. However, when situational ambiguity is high (i.e., it is ambiguous in the situation whether negotiation is acceptable), individuals are less sure about the acceptability of negotiating and will turn to their gender roles to understand how to behave. As a result, as situational ambiguity is reduced, the gender gap in negotiation initiation is reduced. For example, Leibbrandt and List (2015) performed a field experiment in which they randomly assigned half of 2,500 people into a condition in which they either mentioned that wages were potentially negotiable or a condition which had no explicit statement regarding the negotiability of wages. They found that in job contexts where there was no explicit statement (high situational ambiguity), men were more likely to negotiate for a higher wage than women. When there was an explicit statement (low situational ambiguity), this gender effect disappeared. This suggests that when women are given clarity that negotiation is acceptable, they are more willing to negotiate.

6.1.3.2   *Situational Cues*

In addition to examining situational ambiguity, Kugler, Reif, Kaschner, and Brodbeck (2018) also examined the moderating role of situational cues. Specifically, researchers have suggested that highlighting situational cues that are more consistent with the gender role of women than with the gender role of men prior to the negotiation can reduce the perceived inconsistency between women's gender role and the negotiator roles. Indeed, the meta-analysis revealed that situational cues that were congruent with the feminine gender role reduced the gender difference in negotiation initiation. As an example, Small, Gelfand, Babcock, and Gettman (2007) tested whether women were influenced by the language used to frame an upcoming negotiation. Researchers randomly assigned participants to one of three conditions. In one condition, the language was more consistent with the masculine gender role: the task was framed in terms of having an opportunity to negotiate (i.e., "You can negotiate for more if you want," "Many participants negotiate a higher payment," p. 607). In the other condition, the language was more consistent with the feminine gender role, and the task was framed as an opportunity to ask for more (i.e., "You can ask for more if you want," Many participants ask for a higher payment," p. 607). Finally, in the third condition, participants did not receive any cues regarding negotiating or asking. Cues to negotiate increased negotiation propensity overall. However, when the condition was framed as negotiating, a gender gap emerged, with men initiating more than women; when the condition was framed as asking, the gender gap in initiation disappeared.

6.2   Economic Outcomes

Recent research has examined constructs that moderate the relationship between gender and negotiation outcomes (Bowles, Babcock, & McGinn, 2005; Kray, Thompson, & Galinsky, 2001; Kray, Galinsky, & Thompson, 2002). Women expect that acting assertively during a negotiation will provoke negative attributions and backlash. As a result, women tend to use fewer competitive tactics during negotiations which in turn drove lower economic outcomes (Amanatullah & Morris, 2010). These findings have been supported by several meta-analyses. One meta-analysis by Walters, Stuhlmacher, and Meyer (1998) found that men used more competitive tactics than women during the negotiation (e.g., more aggressive offers, more competitive verbal communication). In another meta-analysis by Stuhlmacher and Walters (1999), men performed better financially than women in negotiations. Finally, one of the most comprehensive examinations of gender and economic outcomes is a meta-analysis by Mazei, Huffmeier, Freund, Stuhlmacher, Bilke, and Hertel (2015). They examined 123 effect sizes with over 10,000 subjects and found that men achieved better economic outcomes than women.

While the aforementioned meta-analyses found that men outperformed women in terms of economic outcomes, the effects were small and there was significant variability of the reported effect sizes (i.e., with the prediction interval ranging from −.41 (with women outperforming men) to .80 (with men outperforming women) (see Mazei, Huffmeier, Freund, Stuhlmacher, Bilke, & Hertel, 2015). The result suggests that other factors are at play. Below, we consider three key moderators: negotiator characteristics, the negotiation situation, and specific characteristics of the negotiation.

6.2.1 Negotiator Characteristics

6.2.1.1 Experience

Individuals differ in the levels of experience they have had in negotiation. For example, some individuals have taken a negotiation course in the past, whereas others have not. Negotiation experience helps improve performance (Thompson, 1990; Zerres, Huffmeier, Freund, Backhaus, & Hertel, 2013) and enhances a negotiator's understanding of how to proceed in a negotiation. As a result, women negotiators with experience may be less influenced by their gender role because they have greater clarity of the situation. Indeed, Mazei, Huffmeier, Freund, Stuhlmacher, Bilke, and Hertel (2015) found that negotiation experience moderated the effect of gender on economic outcomes, and the gender gap was smaller when negotiators had past experience negotiating.

6.2.1.2 Power

Another negotiator characteristic is how much power the negotiator holds. Past work has shown that individuals who have a greater sense of power act more agentically and are more action-oriented (Galinsky, Gruenfeld, & Magee, 2003). Research by Hong and van der Wijst (2013) examined how a sense of power moderates the effect of gender on economic outcomes and found that a sense of power reduces the gender gap in negotiation performance. The authors proposed that this occurred because a sense of power emboldens women in particular to negotiate more assertively (e.g., make a stronger first offer), which subsequently results in higher economic outcomes. Furthermore, the authors proposed that a sense of power would not affect men's negotiation behaviors because their gender role was already congruent with assertiveness.

In addition to a sense of power, Stuhlmacher and Walters (1999) found that less power distance between negotiators reduces the size of the gender gap. The authors expected that stereotypical gender differences in economic outcomes would emerge when there was a stereotypical power differential. In line with their predictions, when men possessed more power than women in a negotiation (e.g., men played the supervisor role and women played the subordinate role), men outperformed women. However, when men and women had similar levels of power, the gender gap was diminished.

Interestingly, a recent study by Dannals, Zlatev, Halevy, and Neale (2021) found that possessing negotiation power, namely having a strong outside option (i.e., a strong BATNA), *reinforced* the gender gap because women received greater backlash than men. Specifically, when negotiators had a strong outside option, women performed worse than men. However, when negotiators had a weak outside option, gender differences in performance did not emerge. The authors posited that this occurred because women with strong outside options negotiate more assertively and as a result, their counterparts are more likely to walk away from the bargaining table (i.e., impasse), leaving the full potential value of the deal uncaptured. This research is important because it is one of the few studies that examine impasse rates; by doing so, it eliminates the selection bias of past work examining negotiation performance.

6.2.2   Negotiation Context

In addition to negotiator characteristics, the negotiation context may also influence the effect of gender on economic outcomes. As with the research on negotiation initiation, situational ambiguity and salient gender role cues have been found to moderate the effects of gender on economic outcomes.

6.2.2.1   Situational Ambiguity

Bowles and her colleagues (2005) demonstrated that ambiguity in industry pay can affect the gender gap. The authors compared industries in which there was less clarity about employees' salaries (e.g., telecommunications, commercial banking, real estate finance) to industries where there is more clarity (e.g., private equity and high technology). They demonstrated that in industries in which there was high ambiguity, women were more likely to accept lower offers than men. However, in lower ambiguity industries, this gender difference was eliminated. The meta-analysis by Mazei, Huffmeier, Freund, Stuhlmacher, Bilke, and Hertel (2015) found similar results – the economic advantage of men over women was reduced when information was provided about the size of the zone of possible agreement.

6.2.2.2   Situational Cues

One implication of social role congruity theory is that in circumstances in which the negotiator role and women's gender role is perceived to be more congruent, the gender gap in negotiation performance should be reduced or even reversed (see Wang, Whitson, Anicich, Kray, & Galinsky, 2017, for a review). Several studies have examined this phenomenon.

In general, assertiveness and rationality, stereotypically masculine traits, are associated with effective negotiations. Kray, Thompson, and Galinsky (2001) demonstrated that when those traits were highlighted as important for negotiation success, men achieved better negotiation outcomes than women. However, when individuals were told that communication and listening (stereotypically feminine traits) were integral for negotiation effectiveness, women negotiators set higher goals and performed better than men negotiators.

The ways in which gender roles are emphasized serves as another situational cue. Interestingly, overtly highlighting gender stereotypes in negotiation reduced the gender gap in economic performance. When masculine stereotypes of negotiation were primed in a subtle manner, women performed worse than men. However, when these stereotypes were primed in an overt way, women reacted more strongly against the stereotype (i.e., stereotype reactance), and the gender difference was diminished (Kray, Thompson, & Galinsky, 2001).

6.2.3   Negotiation Characteristics

Other aspects of the negotiation may also influence the effect of gender on economic outcomes. Specifically, we provide an overview of gender negotiation research that has considered the effects of negotiating for oneself versus others, when the negotiation task is cooperative versus competitive, and when the negotiation task is stereotypically feminine versus masculine.

6.2.3.1   *Self versus Other*

Bowles, Babcock, and McGinn (2005) examined whether negotiating on behalf of others also influenced the effects of gender on negotiations. In general, women possess a stronger interdependent self-construal than men, placing a greater focus on maintaining interpersonal relationships and being more responsive to others. As a result, the authors posited that women may feel more positive and achieve more gains when negotiating on behalf of another person versus for themselves. In line with this prediction, women negotiating on behalf of others did better than women negotiating on behalf of themselves. However, no difference emerged between men in the other- and self-negotiation conditions. In a similar study, Amanatullah and Morris (2010) demonstrated that women negotiating on behalf of another person were more assertive during their negotiations because they anticipated less backlash for being assertive, as acting assertively on behalf of another is more congruent with the communal stereotype of women. Overall, a meta-analysis generally confirmed this gender difference (Mazei, Huffmeier, Freund, Stuhlmacher, Bilke, and Hertel, 2015).

6.2.3.2   *Negotiation Tasks*

Research has considered how the cooperative versus competitive nature of the negotiation may also influence the effect of gender on economic performance. Specifically, negotiations can be more distributive (i.e., with only a single issue; zero-sum) or more integrative (i.e., multiple issues; allowing for logrolling or tradeoffs between issues) in nature. Stuhlmacher and Walters (1999) found that men outperformed women more in distributive contexts than in integrative contexts. This finding also falls in line with social role congruity theory – stereotypically masculine traits (e.g., assertiveness) are generally associated with distributive negotiations and stereotypically feminine traits (e.g., cooperativeness) are more congruent with integrative negotiations (Stuhlmacher & Linnabery, 2013; Kray, Thompson, & Lind, 2005).

In another related paper, Kray, Reb, Galinsky, and Thompson (2004) found that actively highlighting gender stereotypes also influenced performance in distributive versus integrative negotiations. When masculine traits were highlighted, higher power negotiators achieved better distributive outcomes. When feminine traits were highlighted, better integrative outcomes were achieved.

Finally, the masculinity or femininity of the negotiation issue can also influence the gender gap. Bear and Babcock (2012) found that, in line with role congruity theory, men achieved better outcomes than women when negotiating over a stereotypically masculine issue (i.e., halogen motorcycle headlights), and that women achieved better outcomes than men when negotiating over a stereotypically feminine issue (i.e., lamp-work jewelry beads).

6.3   Non-Economic Outcomes

The majority of research conducted thus far has focused on initiating economic negotiations and negotiating economic outcomes. However, there is a growing area of work exploring negotiating non-economic outcomes. Below, we review work that examines the effects of gender on career issues (e.g., career advancement and work–family balance) and ethical behavior.

6.3.1   Career Issues

Bowles, Thomason, and Bear (2019) have recently expanded the perspective on gender and negotiations by using inductive methods to understand the types of issues around which women versus men negotiate. Beyond negotiating economic compensation, employees also negotiate role development (e.g., more responsibility) and work–life balance (e.g., work flexibility) related issues. Based on their analyses, three types of negotiation strategies emerged concerning career advancement negotiations: asking, bending, and shaping. The "asking" strategy aligns with a more classic instantiation of negotiating, that is, requesting or proposing a career advancement issue (e.g., a promotion). "Bending" involved requesting or proposing an exception to organizational norms, (e.g., work–family issues: traveling to be with family; being hired into a management-training role instead of the original programming role). Finally, the "shaping" strategy seeks to request or propose an idea that would potentially not only advance one's career, but alter organizational norms (e.g., negotiating changes in a role to take on more responsibility, and suggesting that these changes become an official part of the job description).

Sampling a diverse set of individuals at various stages in their career, and in different industries and sectors (public, private, and nonprofit), the authors find support that, in line with past work (as outlined above), women seem to face more difficulty than men with the "ask." As a result, the authors suggest that women tend to rely more on "bending" strategies than men because unlike the backlash faced by asking, "bending" requests may be one way to manage their pathway within organizations that tend toward stereotypically masculine organizational norms. Specifically, women used bending strategies to negotiate work–life balance – as family matters are more associated with feminine gender roles and contradict stereotypically masculine "ideal worker" norms (Rudman & Mescher, 2013). Also, they use bending strategies to gain access to masculine-stereotypical roles (e.g., leadership roles).

6.3.2   Ethics

Researchers have also examined gender differences in negotiation ethics. In general, research suggest that men behave more unethically than women (Kish-Gephart, Harrison, & Trevino, 2010) and specifically with regards to negotiations, women are less accepting of unethical negotiation tactics, such as deception, than men (Kray & Haselhuhn, 2012). Moreover, women behave more ethically – in an economic bargaining game in which individuals choose whether to lie or tell the truth to a partner, approximately 38% of women lied in order to benefit economically while 55% of men lied (Dreber & Johannesson, 2008).

One reason why women may be likely to use unethical negotiation tactics is because women possess stronger moral identities than men do (see Chapter 8 on discussion on moral identities). In particular, Kennedy,

Kray, and Ku (2017) established that women's strong moral identities reduce their proclivity to rationalize unethical negotiation behavior as acceptable. Unfortunately, because unethical behavior can be economically beneficial, gender differences in decisions to act unethically may partially explain why women do not achieve as good economic outcomes as men in negotiations (Kennedy, Kray, & Ku, 2017).

There are several key moderators to consider. Kennedy, Kray and Ku (2017) explored the role of financial incentives and established that the link between gender and unethical behavior was weakened when there were greater financial incentives to act unethically. This occurred because the incentives decreased the salience of women's moral identity.

Another moderator was the framing of the negotiation. Pierce and Thompson (2018) found that when the negotiation was framed in a cooperative manner (interacting with a partner), men behaved more unethically than women. However, when the negotiation was framed in a competitive manner (a bargaining game), men and women both lied with high frequency.

A final moderator draws again from the literature examining gender differences when women negotiate on behalf of others. While advocating for others improves economic outcomes for women, they also might be more willing to use deception to achieve these better outcomes. Indeed, Kouchaki and Kray (2018) found that when negotiating on behalf of themselves, women were less likely than men to act unethically (e.g., not revealing defects of a car they were selling). However, when they were negotiating on behalf of someone else, women and men were equally likely to deceive their counterparts. Moreover, the authors found that women were more likely to act unethically when they negotiated on behalf of a man (versus woman). They conjectured that this likely occurred because of their assumptions that men (versus women) would prefer that they lie in order to secure a good deal.

6.4   Summary

Research on gender and negotiations has received renewed interest with a focus on three streams of interest: understanding gender differences in negotiation initiation, economic outcomes, and non-economic outcomes. In general, men are more likely to initiate negotiations and achieve better economic outcomes. However, research has considered several situational and negotiator moderators. Overall, the empirical research deeply draws from social role congruity. Importantly, the research has found that situations in which incongruency between the gender role and the negotiator role is diminished for women, the gender gap is weakened, or even reversed.

NOTE

1. The preliminary negotiation research used the terms "sex" and "gender" interchangeably, even though they are separate constructs. Whereas sex consists of the biological attributes of individuals and has historically categorized individuals as either female or male, gender refers to the socially constructed roles of individuals, and the research has generally focused on the categories of men and women. In this chapter, we use the term "gender" rather than "sex."

7   Individual differences

The individual difference approach to negotiations focuses on examining individuals' stable characteristics that reliably influence negotiation processes and outcomes. Individual differences include characteristics such as personality and cognitive abilities, as well as demographic characteristics such as race, gender, and culture. This line of work has gone through several evolutions. In the late 20th century, extensive reviews concluded that the predictive power of individual differences on negotiation processes and outcomes was mixed at best (Bazerman, Curhan, Moore, & Valley, 2000; Thompson, 1990; Lewicki, Litterer, Saunders, & Minton, 1985). The lack of consistent evidence meant that many scholars viewed pursuing individual differences as an avenue of research was unwise (Rubin & Brown, 2013; Hamner, 1980; Lewicki, Litterer, Saunders, & Minton, 1985). As a result, little research was conducted in this area for several decades (for a review, see Sharma, Bottom, & Elfenbein, 2013).

More recently, however, researchers have suggested that more nuance is needed in new research to understand the lack of effects of previous research. This new perspective noted the importance of recognizing the interpersonal complexity of negotiations. Indeed, these calls have encouraged a new wave of research that has considered the effects of individual differences in novel ways. Specifically, three overarching frameworks have been used to understand and examine the effects of individual differences in negotiation: the direct effect approach, the contingency approach, and the dyadic approach. The direct effect approach examines how the individual differences of negotiators directly influence perceptions and behaviors within negotiations. In contrast, the contingency approach considers contingent effects, namely how a combination of a negotiator's characteristics and their situation influence negotiation processes and outcomes. Notably, both the direct effect and contingency approaches have begun to utilize dyadic-level analytics to empirically examine their data. We more fully outline the historical and current perspectives of the individual difference approach below.

7.1   A Rebirth of Individual Differences Research

Given personality's profound effects in other domains, scholars have more recently (in the early 21st century) sought explanations of why past work failed to establish whether and how individual differences may influence negotiation outcomes. Scholars noted that not only was there a limitation in terms of the amount of empirical research to be assessed, there also were potential limitations in the methodology and analysis of the research that was available at the time (Rubin & Brown, 1975; Bottom, Holloway, Miller, Mislin, & Whitford, 2006; Sharma, Bottom, & Elfenbein, 2013). Indeed, more recently, individual differences have generated renewed attention by scholars, with systematic reviews covering both historical and current research (Elfenbein, 2015). The advent of new methodologies and analyses has allowed scholars to present a clearer picture of the effects of individual differences.

7.2   The Direct Effect Approach

Recently, Hillary Elfenbein and her colleagues have begun to re-examine the direct effect of individual differences on negotiation processes and outcomes. The work by Elfenbein and her colleagues, including a meta-analysis by Sharma, Bottom, and Elfenbein (2013), was able to take into account how study designs may influence effect sizes. Since many of the studies have been conducted in laboratory settings, with sample populations limited to university students, the range of individual differences may be smaller, thus obscuring any possible effects (Hamner, 1980; Sharma, Bottom, & Elfenbein, 2013). Indeed, a recent meta-analysis by Sharma, Bottom, and Elfenbein (2013) established that data collected in the field (i.e., often samples of working adults) produced more robust effects than data collected within laboratory settings (e.g., often samples of students).

Beyond these empirical innovations, a review by Elfenbein (2015) provides a structured overview of the state of the field. Specifically, she outlined five distinct categories of individual differences related to negotiation performance: (1) cognitive abilities, such as cognitive intelligence and creativity; (2) personality traits, including the "Big Five" dimensions (extraversion, agreeableness, openness, conscientiousness, and neuroticism) (John, Donahue, & Kentle, 1991); (3) motivations, such as pro-social motivations; (4) expectations and beliefs, such as implicit negotiation beliefs; and (5) personal background characteristics, such as age, race, socio-economic status, and negotiation experience. We outline some of the key findings within each category below.[1]

7.2.1   Key Findings

7.2.1.1   *Cognitive Ability*

Research has established that certain cognitive abilities, such as objective measures of intelligence, are associated with greater individual and joint gain (Sharma, Bottom, & Elfenbein, 2013). However other abilities, such as emotional intelligence, are associated with lower individual gain (Sharma, Bottom, & Elfenbein, 2013; Foo, Elfenbein, Tan, & Aik, 2004). Both high scores on tests of cognitive ability and emotional intelligence were associated with greater subjective value, namely, the perceptual and emotional negotiation consequences (Sharma, Bottom, & Elfenbein, 2013, p. 298; Curhan, Elfenbein, & Xu, 2006). More specifically, emotional intelligence has been associated with greater levels of trust and the desire to negotiate again with counterparts (Kim, Cundiff, & Choi, 2014).

Another cognitive ability is the ability to take perspective, or consider things from another person's perspective. Individual differences in perspective-taking have been shown to predict negotiation processes and outcomes (see Ku, Wang, & Galinsky, 2015, for a review). Researchers have suggested that because negotiators who are high in perspective-taking better understand their counterparts' interests and goals than those who are low in perspective-taking, they are able to craft arguments and make decisions to their advantage (Neale & Bazerman, 1983; Galinsky, Maddux, Gilin, & White, 2008; Gilin, Maddux, Carpenter, & Galinsky, 2013). As a result, negotiators with high perspective-taking ability are less anchored by first offers made by their counterparts (Galinsky & Mussweiler, 2001), claim a larger share of the pie (Neale & Bazerman, 1983; Galinsky, Maddux, Gilin, & White, 2008; Gilin, Maddux, Carpenter,

& Galinsky, 2013), and create more joint value (Galinsky, Maddux, Gilin, & White, 2008; Gilin, Maddux, Carpenter, & Galinsky, 2013; Kemp & Smith, 1994; Trotschel, Huffmeier, Loschelder, Schwartz, & Gollwitzer, 2011). In addition, perspective-takers are less likely to reach an impasse in a negotiation and are more likely to successfully resolve disputes and arbitration (Arriaga & Rusbult, 1998; Long, 1994; Neale & Bazerman, 1983). Interestingly, empathy (i.e., the ability to sense the emotional states of others), a related but distinct ability from perspective-taking, was generally less associated with negotiation processes and outcomes than perspective-taking (see Ku, Wang, & Galinsky, 2015, for a review). One exception was that empathy, but not perspective-taking, was better at deterring unethical behavior (Cohen, 2010).

7.2.1.2   Personality Traits

The effects of the Big Five personality traits have also been examined with regards to negotiation outcomes. Of the Big Five, the most predictive traits were extraversion and agreeableness, with higher scorers tending to perform worse in distributive negotiation settings (Elfenbein, 2015; Barry & Friedman, 1998). One rationale is that highly extraverted individuals, or those who are more sociable and gregarious, tend to be more anchored by their counterparts' first offers, which subsequently reduced their final outcomes (Barry & Friedman, 1998). In terms of agreeableness, highly agreeable people may perform worse in distributive negotiations because they are more concerned about maintaining their interpersonal relationships and will more likely to acquiesce during the negotiation (Elfenbein, 2015). The other personality traits – conscientiousness, neuroticism, and openness – did not seem to substantially influence economic negotiation performance in negotiations.

In addition to the aforementioned personality traits, those who possessed higher positive affect, or the general tendency to experience positive emotional states, tended to have higher levels of individual gain, joint gain, and subjective value than those who possessed lower levels of positive affect (Elfenbein, 2015; Sharma, Bottom, & Elfenbein, 2013).

7.2.1.3   Motivations

Individuals vary in social value orientations, such as how much concern they have for others' outcomes (i.e., pro-social motivations) versus a concern for their own outcomes (i.e., egoistic motivations; Ames & Mason, 2015; Van Lange, De Bruin, Otten, & Joireman, 1997). Past evidence suggests that pro-social value orientations are associated with certain negotiation processes and outcomes (Elfenbein, 2015). One examination found that egoistic motivations predicted greater individual gain (Elfenbein, Curhan, Eisenkraft, Shirako, & Baccaro, 2008). Moreover, a meta-analysis by DeDreu, Weingart, and Kwon (2000) established that negotiators with pro-social motivations are more likely to engage in problem-solving behavior and less contentious behavior in integrative negotiations.

7.2.1.4   Expectations and Beliefs

The expectations individuals hold about themselves influence negotiation outcomes. For example, negotiation self-efficacy, or the belief that one will perform well in a negotiation, has been associated with increased individual gain, joint gain, and subjective value (Elfenbein, 2015; Sharma, Bottom, & Elfenbein, 2013). Interestingly, negotiation self-efficacy has also been associated with the use of deception in negotiations (Gaspar & Schweitzer, 2021).

Another expectation about the self is how much negotiators believe that their negotiation abilities are malleable (negotiation ability can change over time) versus fixed (negotiation ability is stable over time). Kray and Haselhuhn (2007) found that negotiators who believed that negotiation ability was malleable ended up with higher individual and joint outcomes than those who believed negotiation ability was fixed. Interestingly, these expectations seem to have long-term implications; in one of their studies, the researchers measured these expectations about negotiation abilities at the beginning of a semester-long class, and found that these expectations predicted general performance in the course 15 weeks later.

These recent direct effect findings provide evidence that certain individual differences likely influence negotiation outcomes. The recent systematic reviews and analysis of data using meta-analysis techniques have allowed researchers to better parse out individual difference effects.

7.3   The Contingency Approach

In addition to a direct effect of individual differences on negotiation processes and outcomes, researchers have also begun to consider how individual differences may interact with situational factors or other negotiator
characteristics (Thompson, 1990). Past research suggests that negotiation
processes and behaviors are influenced by the combination of aspects of
the situation and the specific characteristics of negotiators (Zechmeister
& Druckman, 1973). We outline several of the findings below.

7.3.1   Cognitive Ability

With regards to contingent approaches of cognitive ability, research
has mainly focused on perspective-taking ability. Specifically, while it
has been established that the cognitive ability to take perspective influences negotiation outcomes, the effects of perspective-taking ability also
are dependent on the relational context. For example, Pierce, Kilduff,
Galinsky, and Sivanathan (2013) established that taking the perspective
of others in competitive contexts engenders the use of unethical negotiation tactics, but taking the perspective of others in cooperative contexts
decreases the use of unethical negotiation tactics. Similarly, Epley, Caruso,
and Bazerman (2006) found that perspective-taking led to more competitive behaviors in competitive negotiation contexts, but not in cooperative
negotiation contexts. The theoretical rationale behind these findings is
that perspective-taking helps individuals understand and navigate their
complex social environments by discerning who is a friend and who is
a foe (Ku, Wang, & Galinsky, 2015). As a result, perspective-takers tend
to act more pro-socially in cooperative contexts, but more competitively
in competitive contexts.

7.3.2   Personality Traits

Dimotakis, Conlon, and Ilies (2012) examined how negotiators' personality traits of agreeableness and the negotiation context (integrative versus
distributive) jointly influence negotiation processes and outcomes. They
found support for the theoretical concept of person–environmental fit –
that when there is a strong fit between an individual's characteristics and
their environment, more positive outcomes will occur (Kristof-Brown,
Zimmerman, & Johnson, 2005). Specifically, the authors found that negotiators high in agreeableness were more engaged (as measured by greater

physiological arousal), exhibited greater positive affect, and were more persistent during negotiations in integrative versus distributive settings. In turn, these results were positively associated with better performance in the negotiation.

Another set of studies using the contingency approach of personality traits focused on trait positive affect. Anderson and Thompson (2004) examined the role of negotiators' trait positive affect and their levels of power (i.e., whether they possessed more power than their counterparts) on levels of mutual levels of trust and joint economic outcomes. In their studies, dyads negotiated in a simulation in which one party was more dependent on the other party to reach a deal; or in other words, one party had more power than the other party. The researchers demonstrated that the positive affect of high-power negotiators (versus low-power negotiators) was a better predictor of dyads' levels of trust and produced higher joint gains than the positive affect of less powerful negotiators. Interestingly, trait positive affect had predictive power even when controlling for negotiators' levels of trait cooperativeness and communicativeness. The authors theorized that these findings occurred because powerful negotiators' positive affect shaped the negotiation setting as positive and trusting.

7.3.3   Motivations

A meta-analysis by DeDreu, Weingart, and Kwon (2000) included 28 negotiation studies and tested the roles of two factors: negotiators' resistance to yielding (high versus low) and social motives (pro-social versus egoistic). Negotiators who have a high resistance to yielding tend to be less willing to make concessions and to 'give in' to their counterparts. One way researchers have encouraged high resistance to yielding in studies has been to set more ambitious (versus less ambitious) aspiration points or reservation points – in other words, it is more difficult to come to agreements when there is a high resistance to yielding. The researchers established that negotiators achieved higher joint outcomes when they possessed a pro-social rather than an egoistic motivation, but only in contexts in which a resistance to yielding was high or unknown versus low. The authors noted that these findings support the Dual Concern Theory (see Chapter 1 for details), as compared to egoistic negotiators, pro-social negotiators who have a high resistance to yielding are more willing to engage in problem-solving and exchange information that allows negotiators to discover integrative solutions. In contrast, pro-social negotiators who possess a low resistance to yielding are too willing to make unilateral concessions and thus are more likely to miss integrative solutions.

7.3.4   Expectations and Beliefs

Stevens and Gist (1997) demonstrated the role of self-efficacy in responding to negotiation training sessions. In their study, participants received negotiation content training, completed a first negotiation, received a post-training intervention, and then completed a second negotiation seven weeks after the intervention session. In the post-training intervention, participants received advice regarding their first negotiation via a self-management (i.e., use the feedback to improve your skills) or goal attainment (i.e., use the feedback to achieve your best outcome) lens. The combination of trait self-efficacy and the post-training condition influenced the second negotiation outcome. High self-efficacy individuals did better than low self-efficacy individuals when they completed the goal attainment intervention because high self-efficacy individuals were less likely to cognitively withdraw from the situation. However, self-efficacy did not influence performance when participants received the self-management intervention.

Research has also established individual differences in trait self-efficacy as a moderator. Volkema and colleagues (2013) examined how two individual difference factors, (1) feelings of self-efficacy and (2) the ability to recognize the situations and opportunities to negotiate, jointly predicted intentions to initiate negotiations. Specifically, they found that opportunity recognition was significantly associated with the likelihood of initiating a negotiation, and this relationship was strengthened by feelings of self-efficacy.

7.4   Dyadic Approaches

Past examinations of whether person-level factors (e.g., individual characteristics) predict group-level effects (i.e., dyadic- and team-level outcomes) have had limited success. This is somewhat unsurprising since negotiations are inherently interpersonal and dyadic in nature. Past empirical investigations have not adequately taken these considerations into account and there has been an empirical mismatch in levels of past individual difference research. For example, scholars have noted that examining the dyadic data at the individual level is "theoretically deficient" (Krasikova & LeBreton, 2012, p. 741). In order to address this limitation, researchers have utilized methods that allow them to more clearly examine the dyadic effects within their models. These models include the social relation model and the relational process model, which are described in more detail below.

7.4.1 Social Relations Model

One strategy to address these empirical limitations has been to use the Social Relations Model, a mathematical method that allows researchers to separate out person-level effects and dyad-level effects (Kenny & La Voie, 1984). In the context of negotiations, this method allows researchers to "disentangle the role of individual differences in the context of interpersonal processes that are inherently dyadic" (Elfenbein, Curhan, Eisenkraft, Shirako, & Baccaro, 2008, p. 1464).

In one examination, using the Social Relations Model, Elfenbein and her colleagues (2008) looked at the consistency of results of individuals across a series of negotiations. The researchers first measured a host of individual characteristics and then separated negotiators into groups of four to five individuals. Individuals subsequently negotiated in pairs across a variety of simulations until each had negotiated with every individual within their group. A robust effect emerged of individual differences on negotiation outcomes, with individual differences explaining almost 50% of objective performance (e.g., economic outcomes) and 19% of subjective performance (e.g., how much their counterparts liked them). Moreover, in line with the review by Elfenbein (2015), the researchers found that the individual differences that best predicted subjective and objective negotiation outcomes included negotiation self-efficacy (i.e., the belief that one will perform well in a negotiation), positive affect (a general tendency to experience positive moods), and a concern for one's own outcome.

7.4.2 Relational Process Model and the Person-as-Situation Approach

Another interesting new theoretical and empirical perspective, the Relational Process Model (RPM), focuses on the dyadic nature of individual differences (Elfenbein, 2021). As negotiation is an interdependent, relational context, it is important to go beyond the traditional view that examines individual negotiators in isolation, and understand how the dyadic nature of negotiations means that there are sets of "complex behavioral dynamics" to consider. The traditional view states that individual differences influence individual behaviors, which in turn influence negotiation outcomes. However, Elfenbein (2021) theorizes that the combination of the individual differences of the focal negotiator and counterpart(s) affect both the focal and counterpart(s)' behaviors. In turn, these combinations then influence both individual and joint outcomes.

Elfenbein goes on to describe a negotiation process of interaction in five stages. First, individual characteristics influence the decision to negotiate in the first place; for example, individuals may be more inclined to want to negotiate with those that share similar characteristics (e.g., extraverted people are drawn to other extraverted individuals; Byrne, 1962; McPherson, Smith-Lovin, & Cook, 2001). Second, individual characteristics may influence expectations of others' behaviors. For example, research has demonstrated that prior to the negotiation, individuals set higher aspirations against female versus male counterparts (Bowles, Babcock, & McGinn, 2005). Third, drawing from the person-as-situation approach, individual characteristics create a distinctive signature for each negotiator and this signature can serve as a situational cue in which a counterpart's strong personality (e.g., high extraversion) may influence a negotiator's responses (e.g., making small talk). Fourth, as a response, the negotiators' behaviors influence each other and "co-create their situation as the bargaining stage is set," which has implications for outcomes in negotiations. For example, a study by Kelley and Stahelski (1970) examined dyads in a distributive negotiation. In dyads in which both individuals were high in competitiveness or both low in competitiveness, final outcomes tend to be more evenly split. However, mixed pairs (one high in competitiveness and one low in competitiveness) tended to yield more one-sided outcomes. This model has provided a framework for new research and has led to many interesting recent studies.

More recent empirical works have considered the dyadic nature of individual differences in negotiations, and specifically have used the person-as-situation approach to provide greater insights. For example, Wilson, DeRue, Matta, Howe, and Conlon (2016) examined the Big Five personality traits of extroversion and agreeableness in negotiating dyads

and proposed that personality similarity would influence a host of negotiation outcomes. They found that negotiators who were similar along
these traits reached agreements more quickly, perceived less relationship
conflict, and possessed more positive impressions of their counterparts,
and that these effects were driven by more positive emotional displays
during the negotiation. Importantly, the results not only emerged when
dyads were both high in agreeableness and extraversion, but also when
dyads were both low in agreeableness and extraversion.

Another study on personality similarity in negotiation dyads examined
the effects of Machiavellianism and the type of communication used to
negotiate. Machiavellianism is the tendency for individuals to seek personal gain through deception and manipulation, and individuals with high
Machiavellianism are considered to be more controlling and confident in
negotiation situations. While negotiators high in Machiavellianism are
more likely to initiate negotiations (Kapoutsis, Volkema, & Nikolopoulos,
2013) the evidence that they claim more value is mixed (Huber & Neale,
1986; Greenhalgh & Neslin, 1983). As such, Fry (1985) proposed that the
effects of dyadic Machiavellianism may be moderated by communication
medium. Specifically, Fry paired together two negotiators who were low
in Machiavellianism, two negotiators who were high in Machiavellianism,
or a mixed-Machiavellianism group (one high and one low). In addition,
the authors either had these pairs negotiate face-to-face or negotiate being
able to hear each other, but not being able to see each other. Fry found that
the mixed-Machiavellian pairs negotiating face-to-face performed the
worst and posited that this occurred because the low Machiavellianism
negotiator in these pairs felt greater apprehension and was thus less likely
to generate feasible offers that helped the dyad come to a deal.

In another empirical piece that tested the person-as-situation theoretical
perspective, Elfenbein, Eisenkraft, Curhan, and DiLalla (2018) introduced
a novel methodology by comparing and contrasting how twins (i.e.,
both identical and fraternal) negotiate. By comparing the negotiation
performance of twins, the researchers were able to separate out effects
driven purely by the negotiators' individual-level characteristics from
those driven by the dyadic effects of the negotiators and their counterparts. Specifically, participants negotiated several times with counterparts. Concurrently, the participants' twins negotiated several times with
the counterparts' twins. This design allowed the researchers to estimate
effects without carry-over effects or the effects that may occur from

repeated negotiations (i.e., aspects of the first interaction may influence aspects of the second interaction). The authors drew from Greek philosopher Heraclitus to explain this quandary, that "a person cannot step into the same river twice" (Elfenbein, Eisenkraft, Curhan, & DiLalla, 2018, p. 90). By using twins who share genetic similarity, the authors argued that "although it is never possible to step in the same river twice, the independent experiences of twins may reveal what happens when two similar people step into two similar rivers" (Elfenbein, Eisenkraft, Curhan, & DiLalla, 2018, p. 91). The authors found that as compared to the individual characteristics, the dyadic effects explained more variation in negotiation outcomes. However, the individual characteristics explained more variation than the dyadic effects with regards to the subjective negotiation outcomes.

In sum, recent research suggests that it is important to consider individual differences of both the focal negotiators, but also the individual differences of their counterparts. These dyadic effects explain a significant amount of variance and suggest that continuing to consider these dyadic effects is important for painting the whole portrait.

7.5   Summary

Our review outlines historical and current perspectives of the individual difference approach to negotiations. In the late 20th century, a number of studies emerged examining the effects of individual differences on negotiation outcomes, with often mixed findings. For example, whereas scholars have suggested that demographic characteristics, such as gender, influence negotiation outcomes, a clear pattern of findings did not emerge (see Thompson, 1990, for a review). As Elfenbein (2015, p. 131) noted, these inconclusive findings had a "chilling effect on research about individual differences, and for decades the topic was largely abandoned."

More recently, individual difference research has experienced renewed interest and our review in this chapter outlines three overarching approaches that have been used. First, examinations of the direct effect approach have established more consistent effects, demonstrating that several categories of negotiator individual differences are associated with negotiation perceptions and behaviors. Second, support for the contingency approach is growing, with evidence that negotiators' individual characteristics and the negotiation context interact to influence negotiation processes and outcomes. Finally, recent empirical work has utilized dyadic approaches to examining negotiation data. These approaches will likely continue to encourage innovative work in the realm of individual differences and negotiation in the future.

NOTE

1.   Given the robust areas of research, we fully review the research on culture in Chapter 9 and the research on gender in Chapter 6. We also consider the effects of individual differences in moral thinking (i.e., moral identity; Morse & Cohen, 2019) in Chapter 8.

8   Ethics

In this chapter, we discuss the various frameworks and assumptions related to ethics and negotiations. We begin by outlining types of negotiator unethical behavior and outlining the perceived acceptability of certain negotiation tactics and behaviors. Then, we explore different theoretical perspectives regarding people's motivation to use ethically questionable tactics in the negotiation process. Next, we then discuss the contextual and negotiator factors that affect ethical actions in the context of negotiations. Fourth, we provide an overview of the research examining the consequences of unethical behavior. Finally, we discuss the literature outlining the ways to curtail unethical behavior in negotiations.

8.1   Types of Unethical Behavior

Unethical behavior is behavior that is viewed as morally unacceptable to society (Mayer, Aquino, Greenbaum, & Kuenzi, 2012). Unethical behavior can take many forms, and researchers have examined a wide variety of unethical behavior in negotiations. There has been a particular focus on understanding deception, and recently researchers have offered a framework to understand deception in negotiations. Specifically, Gaspar, Methasani, and Schweitzer (2019) have broken deception in negotiations down into three dimensions: content, intentionality, and activity. In terms of content, two categories of unethical behavior have been examined: unethical behavior around the information pertinent to the negotiation, and unethical behavior as it relates to emotions. An example of informational-based unethical behavior is when negotiators lie about their needs or preferences. An example of emotion-based unethical behavior is when negotiators act angry when they are in fact not. In terms of intentionality, negotiators can lean toward self-interest and maximizing their own outcomes or pro-social and focusing on the other party's outcomes. Finally, researchers have delineated deceptive activities: lies of commission (active misstatements), lies of omission (omitted information that conveys a false belief) or paltering (using honest statements to mislead the counterparts).

8.2   Acceptability of Tactics and Behaviors

While many of the actions described above have been discussed as unethical behavior, there is still a great deal of ambiguity about what is "right" and "wrong" when it comes to negotiation behavior. On one hand, some scholars have encouraged the development of honest and moral practices in negotiations, in line with the prescriptions of philosophical ethics (Dees & Cramton, 1991; 1995; Trevino, den Nieuwenboer, & Kish-Gephart, 2014). On the other hand, other scholars assert that certain behaviors, such as deception, may at times be considered morally acceptable (Strudler, 1995).

To help resolve this confusion, researchers have empirically evaluated the perceived acceptability and ethicalness of certain negotiation tactics and behaviors (Lewicki & Stark, 1996; Robinson, Lewicki, & Donahue, 2000; Applbaum, 1996). For example, Robinson, Lewicki, and Donahue (2000) developed the "Self-reported Inappropriate Negotiation Strategies" (SINS) scale, in which MBA students were asked to rate the (in)appropriateness of 30 negotiation tactics. In a factor analysis of these ratings, five tactics emerged: traditional competitive bargaining (e.g., aggressive first offers); attacking an opponent's network (e.g., attempting to get the counterpart fired); misrepresentation (e.g., misrepresenting aspects of your side to make sure you look stronger); misuse of information (e.g., gaining information about the other side via bribes); and false promises (e.g., promising to give future concessions when you do not really intend to).

Of these tactics, individuals generally viewed the traditional competitive bargaining tactics as acceptable. However, the other tactics, such as misrepresentation and false promises, were generally considered inappropriate. Moreover, compared to lies of commission, lies of omission are considered less serious (Schweitzer & Croson, 1999; Dees & Cramton, 1991).

In any case, both practitioners (Adler, 2007) and scholars (Aquino, 1998; Koning, Van Dijk, Van Beest, & Steinel, 2010) recognize that unethical behavior is relatively common in negotiation. Due to its ubiquitous nature, understanding the causes of unethical behavior in negotiations has been a common area of research.

8.3   Causes of Unethical Behavior

8.3.1   Theoretical Perspectives

One of the key questions researchers have asked is why negotiators act ethically or unethically. Two key theoretical perspectives have emerged: the relational choice perspective and the bounded ethicality perspective.

8.3.1.1   *Self-Interest and the Rationality Assumption*

One perspective contends that negotiators use ethically questionable tactics because they are self-interested. Drawing from the *rational choice model* discussed in Chapter 1, the ethics literature assumes that negotiators are rational and seek to maximize their utility (Bazerman, Curhan, Moore, & Valley, 2000; Adler, 2007; Carson, Wokutch, & Murrmann, 1982). An implication of this rational choice model is the notion that negotiators will act unethically, if it is beneficial to them, regardless of whether their behavior harms the other party (Gaspar & Schweitzer, 2013; Gneezy, 2005). In line with this perspective, Lewicki (1983) suggests that negotiators decide whether to act unethically using an analysis that takes into account the perceived costs and benefits of using deception.

Indeed, researchers have argued that deception is an important strategy for increasing one's own outcome (Lewicki, Litterer, Saunders, & Minton, 1985; O'Connor & Carnevale, 1997; Murnighan, Babcock, Thompson, & Pillutla, 1999; Schweitzer & Croson, 1999). For example, misrepresenting information in a negotiation may allow you to gain information and make offers that will benefit you or gain your counterpart's trust. Similarly, Tenbrunsel (1998) and Tenbrunsel and Messick (1999) found that negotiators who possess strong incentives to cheat are more likely to act unethically. In one study, Tenbrunsel (1998) developed a scenario in which two partners were negotiating the dissolution of a business partnership, and participants either had a strong incentive ($100) or a weak incentive ($1) to misrepresent information to the arbitrator. Those that were in the strong incentive condition were more likely to misrepresent information than those in the weak incentive condition.

8.3.1.2   Bounded Ethicality

The rational choice model suggests intentionality with regards to unethical behavior – that negotiators are opportunistic and deliberately lie or manipulate the situation during the negotiation process to maximize gains. However, individuals do not always act in line with this theorizing. Indeed, participants within laboratory studies often choose not to deceive their counterparts, even when the chances of getting caught are low and there are clear economic benefits from the deception (Gneezy, 2005). Similarly, Boles, Croson, and Murnighan (2000) determined that the frequency of deception is not in line with what the rational choice model would predict; in a repeated ultimatum game, proposers and responders were only deceptive approximately 60 times, out of the total 440 opportunities to deceive their counterparts. Moreover, while the theory behind the rational choice model suggests that individuals are generally motivated to deceive others, research suggests that many are averse to engaging in deception (Erat & Gneezy, 2012; Lundquist, Ellingsen, Gribbe, & Johannesson, 2009).

A more recent theoretical perspective, which suggests that negotiators do not realize when they act in ways that may be considered unethical, may explain these findings. This perspective, called *bounded ethicality* (Messick & Bazerman, 1996; Chugh, Bazerman, & Banaji, 2005), suggests that ethical decision making is largely subconscious. Because of subconscious processes, individuals tend to fall prey to "systematic and predictable ethical errors" (Kern & Chugh, 2009, p. 378).

In sum, the assumption within the rational choice perspective assumes that ethical choices are completed intentionally, whereas the assumption within the bounded ethicality perspective is that negotiators act from automaticity and without much cognitive deliberation.

8.3.2   Situational Cues

Situational cues may play a central role in how negotiators cognitively perceive the situation. These perceptions, in turn, can influence whether or not negotiators act unethically. We outline several cues below.

8.3.2.1   *Loss versus Gain Frames*

Prospect Theory (Kahneman & Tversky, 1979) posits that individuals are more affected by losses than by gains. Moreover, the effects of framing are immediate and automatic in nature. Research by Kern and Chugh (2009) draws from this theory and establishes that loss frames (versus gain frames) increase negotiators' propensity to lie to their counterparts, and that this effect emerges only when there was time pressure to close the deal. The moderating role in time pressure suggests that automatic or subconscious processes, rather than deliberate processes, were driving the effects.

8.3.2.2   *Competitive versus Cooperative*

Another aspect of negotiation that might influence unethical behaviors is whether the negotiation is framed or perceived as primarily competitive or cooperative. In general, the process of negotiation itself is viewed as a competitive context (Thompson & Hastie, 1990), and research has shown that contexts viewed as competitive in nature can spur unethical actions. For example, distributive negotiations can drive unethical tactics by negotiators who want to gain advantage (DeRue, Conlon, Moon, & Willaby, 2009). In another study, negotiators who viewed the negotiation as a conflict were more likely to act unethically (Aquino, 1998; Schweitzer, DeChurch, & Gibson, 2005). Congruently, an economic game called the "Wall Street" game (i.e., competitively framed) resulted in greater defection in a prisoner's dilemma game than the same game called the "Community" game (i.e., cooperatively framed; Liberman, Samuels, & Ross, 2004). One line of reasoning to explain these findings is that unethical actions in response to competition are intentional, as negotiators are attempting to protect themselves from being exploited (Pierce, Kilduff, Galinsky, & Sivanathan, 2013). However, other lines of reasoning take the bounded rationality perspective, arguing that competition winnows negotiators' views so that they no longer understand how their unethical actions can harm others (Rees, Tenbrunsel, & Bazerman, 2019).

8.3.2.3   Uncertainty

A typical negotiation contains many elements of uncertainty. For example, there might be uncertainty around the market value of a company's inventory or the value of a partnership. Research shows that when there is uncertainty around aspects of the negotiation, negotiators will provide themselves leeway to strategically improve their own side, sometimes through the use of ethically questionable behaviors (Schweitzer & Hsee, 2002; Gaspar & Schweitzer, 2013). In one study by Tenbrunsel (1998), negotiators were either certain or uncertain about an estimate regarding their projects and the potential market share that they could command. Uncertain negotiators, compared to certain ones, provided more aggressive and less honest estimates regarding the market share. Researchers have argued that this deception occurs in uncertain situations because the ambiguity around what is right and wrong allows individuals to rationalize their unethical actions (Kreve, 2016). Moreover, uncertainty biases individuals to focus on their own desires (Bazerman, Tenbrunsel, & Wade-Benzoni, 1998), blinding them from how their actions may harm the other side (Rees, Tenbrunsel, & Bazerman, 2019).

8.3.2.4   Media Richness

Technology has changed the way we negotiate, and research suggests that the type of media negotiators use when negotiating may influence unethical behavior. Computer-mediated, video-mediated, and face-to-face interaction differ in the types of information they transmit between the parties. In general, face-to-face interactions provide the most richness, allowing people to see and hear and respond to others quickly. There is some research that suggests that negotiators are more likely to lie when using non-visual mediums (e.g., chat and email) than face-to-face and video communication mediums. It is suggested that this occurs because it is harder to establish trust in non-visual mediums than in visual mediums (Ebner, 2015).

8.3.2.5   Agents

Negotiations often include the use of agents or individuals who represent a party at the negotiation table, for example, lawyers and real estate agents. Research suggests that the use of agents increases the use of unethical behavior at the negotiation table (Rubin & Sander, 1988). The rationale is that agents, who feel pressure to perform well, will use deception as a tactic to improve the outcomes of the party they are representing (Robertson & Rymon, 2001). Moral disengagement also seems to be a key mechanism driving the effects: acting as an agent for a constituent who communicates more lax (versus more strict) attitudes toward unethical conduct results in individuals justifying their transgressions as acceptable and in turn, increased use of unethical negotiation tactics (Aaldering, Zerres, & Steinel, 2020).

8.3.2.6 Teams

Research has established that unethical behavior occurs more in team negotiations than in individual negotiations (Aykac, Wilken, Jacob, & Prime, 2017). In one study run by Cohen and her colleagues (2009), a party had the opportunity to lie to another party in an economic bargaining game. Three-on-three parties exhibited more lying than one-on-one interactions, even though the incentives to lie were extremely low ($1 per person). This finding was thought to occur because in teams, unethical behavior may be seen as more normative and practical for group success (Gino, Ayal, & Ariely, 2009).

8.3.3 Negotiator Characteristics

Beyond situational cues, there is also evidence that certain characteristics of the negotiators play a role in ethical decision making. In some cases, a combination of individual differences and situational factors work together to influence levels of unethical behavior in negotiations.

8.3.3.1 Power

The level of power negotiators hold can influence unethical behavior (Tenbrunsel & Messick, 2001). For example, negotiators who possess more power (e.g., have more information) will lie more (Boles, Croson, & Murnighan, 2000; Crott, Kayser, & Lamm, 1980). While some researchers suggest that high-power negotiators (i.e., those who possess alternative deals) are opportunistic and intentionally act unethically (Malhotra & Gino, 2011), other researchers suggest that high-power individuals utilize more heuristic and automatic processing (Keltner, Gruenfeld, & Anderson, 2003), and thus are more likely to act unethically because they are overlooking the interests of their counterparts (Murnighan, Cantelon, & Elyashiv, 2001).

8.3.3.2   Moral Character

Recently, scholars have focused on the effects of various traits related to moral identity, or "one's general tendency to think, feel, and behave in ways associated with ethical and unethical behavior" (Morse & Cohen, 2019, p. 12). For example, research has examined the effects of guilt proneness, which is the tendency to experience negative feelings about ethical transgressions. Researchers have found that negotiators who were high in guilt proneness, an aspect of moral character, were less likely to condone the use of unethical negotiation tactics than those who were low in guilt proneness (Cohen, Panter, Turan, & Kim, 2014) and less likely to act in a unethical manner (Aquino, Freeman, Reed II, Lim, & Felps, 2009; Kennedy, Kray, & Ku, 2017).

Two other aspects of moral identity are empathy, the ability to consider others' feelings, and perspective-taking, the cognitive ability to walk in others' shoes (Ku, Wang, & Galinsky, 2015; Cohen, 2010) demonstrated that individuals high in empathy, but not perspective-taking, were less likely to use tactics such as misrepresentation and inappropriate information-gathering in their negotiation. Empathy is thought to discourage these behaviors because it is harder to harm others if you are actively considering their feelings. The research around perspective-taking seems more nuanced, and the empirical results are more dependent on the situational context. Work by Pierce and colleagues (Pierce, Kilduff, Galinsky, & Sivanathan, 2013) demonstrated that in cooperative contexts, perspective-taking fosters pro-social impulses and cooperative behavior. However, in competitive contexts, perspective-taking leads to unethical behavior to protect negotiators from harm.

8.3.3.3   Social Value Orientation

Messick and McClintock (1968) developed the concept of social value orientation, which is individuals' preferences for pro-self distributions versus pro-social distributions in interdependent situations. Research has found that pro-self negotiators exhibit more unethical behavior than pro-social negotiators. For example, as compared to pro-social negotiators, pro-self negotiators are more likely to act strategically and lie about private information (O'Connor & Carnevale, 1997; Steinel, Utz, & Koning, 2010). This effect is particularly prominent when negotiators are in the domain of losses, suggesting that individual differences interact with situational factors (Reinders Folmer & De Cremer, 2012).

8.3.3.4   Affect

The affect of the negotiator has been found to influence deception in negotiations. Positive emotions and moods have been associated with cooperative behavior in negotiations, whereas negative emotions and moods
have been associated with competitive behavior (Barry & Oliver, 1996).
With particular respect to unethical behavior, negotiators who experience
negative emotions are more likely to engage in deceptive behavior. Envy
and anxiety, for example, have both been found to increase deception in
negotiations (Moran & Schweitzer, 2008). Even emotions that are not
triggered by the negotiation situation itself, that is, incidental emotions,
can spur deception in negotiations (Moran & Schweitzer, 2008).

8.3.3.5   Gender

A review of the literature by Jazaieri and Kray (2020) suggests that
there are gender differences in terms of unethical behavior. Specifically,
research suggests that men tend to have more lenient ethical standards
than women, and as a result, are more willing to use deceptive tactics
in negotiations (Haselhuhn & Wong, 2012; Kennedy, Kray, & Ku, 2017;
Kray, Thompson, & Lind, 2005). One theoretical perspective is that this
gender difference occurs because women, as compared to men, possess
stronger moral identities, which suppress unethical negotiating behavior
(Kennedy, Kray, & Ku, 2017). In another paper by Lee and colleagues
(2017), researchers used an evolutionary argument for why men use
deceit more often. They found that the greatest usage of unethical tactics
was when men were negotiating with attractive men. They posited that
this occurred because male negotiators felt more intrasexual competition
with same-sexed partners, and thus were more likely to deceive them to
gain an advantage.

Research has also examined the question of which gender is more likely
to be deceived. In one paper, women were more likely to be deceived than
men because people stereotyped the women as being more easily misled
than the men (Kray, Kennedy, & Van Zant, 2014).

Finally, researchers have begun to examine key moderators of this gender
effect. Kouchaki and Kray (2018) found that women negotiating on behalf
of others versus negotiating on their own behalf were more willing to use
deceptive tactics in their negotiation. This occurred because the women
felt anticipatory guilt that they would let their constituents down. Men,

on the other hand, were equally likely to use deceptive tactics when negotiating regardless of whether they were negotiating on behalf of others or themselves.

Another set of recent research goes back to the assumptions about competition and cooperation in a negotiation (Pierce & Thompson, 2018). Whereas men tend to view negotiations as a competitive and zero-sum context, women tend to view them as a cooperative context in which both sides can win. This perspective led to men using more unethical tactics than women. However, this gender difference could be eliminated: placing women in a competitive context (versus a cooperative context) resulted in greater unethical behavior, whereas placing men in a cooperative context led to fewer unethical decisions.

8.4   Curtailing Unethical Behavior

A review of the causes of unethical behavior suggests that there are certain ways to curtail unethical behavior. For example, reframing a loss situation into a gain game frame might reduce the likelihood that individuals will act unethically. Similarly, framing a negotiation in terms of cooperation may curb decisions to act unethically. In addition, given the potentially deleterious outcomes that negotiators have if they are deceived, researchers have examined specific tactics negotiators can use to curtail the potential use of unethical behavior by their counterparts.

8.4.1   Questioning

One way to reduce lies in negotiations is asking your counterparts direct questions. Schweitzer and Croson (1999) demonstrated that negotiators who were asked direct questions were less likely to lie than those who were not asked any questions. In one of their studies, a potential buyer of a car asked a direct question to the seller of a car about the mechanical condition of the car. Sellers who were asked this direct question were significantly more likely to reveal that the car had a mechanical problem than those who were not asked a direct question. Minson and colleagues (Minson, Ruedy, & Schweitzer, 2011) went on to examine how the types of questions are important in curtailing lies. General questions, such as "what can you tell me about your car?" were less effective in curtailing lies than more specific questions with positive assumptions, "the car has not been in an accident, correct?" Moreover, positive assumption questioning was less effective than negative assumption questioning, namely, "How many accidents has the car been in?"

8.4.2 Ethical Salience

The salience of ethical climate has also been shown to deter deception in negotiations. In a study by Aquino (1998), negotiators were either working for an automotive company or as a supplier of component parts. In the high ethical saliency condition, participants working for the automotive company were told that the company prided itself on "being fair and honest in its business dealings," and were given information that the culture did not condone deceptive tactics. Participants in the low ethical saliency condition were not given any information about the culture of the organization. Those in the high ethical saliency condition were less likely to use deception in the negotiation than those in the low ethical saliency condition, and as a result, the outcomes were more equal between the two negotiating parties.

8.4.3 Contingency Contracts

A contingent contract is an agreement in which the outcome depends on a future event. For example, an author and a publisher might agree that the author receives 10% of future sales. Contingency contracts are considered to be a good way to protect oneself from dishonest negotiators and to diagnose deception (Adler, 2007). In a classic *Harvard Business Review* article (Bazerman & Gillespie, 1999), Max Bazerman noted that contingency contracts are a good way to test the other parties' beliefs in their stated positions. For example, a clothing buyer who does not believe that a manufacturer is telling the truth about their stated speed of a clothing shipment may introduce a contingency contract that places the shipment payment on the party that is correct about the final shipment date.

8.5 Consequences of Unethical Behavior

While research has mainly focused on understanding the causes of unethical behavior, there is also work examining the consequences of unethical behavior (Gaspar, Methasani, & Schweitzer, 2019). Specifically, research has attempted to understand the effects of unethical behavior in negotiations on the targets and actors of unethical behavior.

8.5.1 Target Outcomes

Earlier work examining unethical behavior made a clear assumption that deception causes significant harm to the targets of deception in the negotiation (Schweitzer, Hershey, & Bradlow, 2006; Adler, 2007). Indeed, negotiators do tend to gain some benefits from deceiving the other side, at the expense of the other side (see Gunia, 2019 for a review). However, more recent work has challenged the ubiquitously harmful nature of unethical behavior. In particular, research established that lies can mislead but also benefit targets, that is, pro-social lies. This work's theoretical assumption deviates from the assumptions of the self-interest and bounded rationality perspectives and suggests that actors will tell pro-social lies when it provides benefits to the target (Gaspar, Levine, & Schweitzer, 2015). For example, studies by Levine and Schweitzer (2014; 2015) demonstrate that individuals in economic games are willing to pro-socially lie to targets, even though this leads to a lower payoff than they would have received if they were honest.

8.5.2 Actor Outcomes

8.5.2.1 Trust

In general, deception during negotiation reduces trust in the deceiver. For example, negotiators who use truthful statements to mislead a counterpart (known as paltering) or who lie by commission are trusted less than those who are honest (Rogers, Zeckhauser, Gino, Norton, & Schweitzer, 2017). Congruently, those who were not truthful about their emotions, such as faking anger (Cote, Hideg, & Van Kleef, 2013; Campagna, Mislin, Kong, & Bottom, 2016), were less trusted. Acts of deception are harmful long-term, as trust is never fully restored after the deception is revealed (Schweitzer, Hershey, & Bradlow, 2006).

However, there are instances in which deception can engender trust (Levine & Schweitzer, 2014; 2015). Namely, research has established that lies that mislead but benefit targets, that is, pro-social lies, increased trust in the deceiver by both targets and observers of lies. Specifically, targets of a pro-social lie passed more money (an instantiation of trust) in a trust game to the deceiver. In addition, the type of trust matters – pro-social deception increased benevolent-based trust (i.e., the deceiver had positive intentions), but not integrity-based trust (i.e., the deceiver has an honest reputation).

8.5.2.2 Behavioral Outcomes

While unethical behavior has been shown to benefit the deceiver, research has also outlined the negative ramifications for the deceiver. For example, research has demonstrated that whereas paltering can provide a distributive advantage, it also increases the likelihood of an impasse in a negotiation (Rogers, Zeckhauser, Gino, Norton, & Schweitzer, 2017). Honest and dishonest reputations also affect negotiation outcomes. Research demonstrated that individuals use tougher tactics when they are negotiating with a person who has a reputation of being a liar versus being honest, in order to protect themselves from being taken advantage of (Glick & Croson, 2001). Additional research has delineated between honest and friendly reputations. In general, negotiators with honest reputations were less likely to be lied to than those with friendly reputations. However, it seems that those who hold honest reputations are held to a higher standard – when negotiators with honest reputations used deceptive tactics (in a manner incongruent to their reputation), they were *more* likely to be lied to as compared to negotiators with friendly reputations (SimanTov-Nachlieli, Har-Vardi, & Moran, 2020).

8.6   Summary

In this chapter, we outlined the growing literature on negotiations and unethical behavior. We summarized the types of unethical behavior that are prevalent in negotiation contexts, and then the acceptability of certain negotiation tactics and behaviors. We outlined the different theoretical perspectives for why negotiators use ethically questionable tactics in negotiation. Next, we discussed how certain contextual factors and negotiator factors affect ethical actions in the context of negotiations. Then, we provided an overview of the research examining the consequences of unethical behavior. Finally, we discuss the literature outlining the ways to curtail unethical behavior in negotiations.

9   Culture

Culture is what is created when a particular group of people possesses a mutual meaning system (Markus & Kitavama, 2010) and share a unique set of values, beliefs, norms, and behaviors (Adair & Brett, 2005). The study of culture and negotiation has been led by Jeanne Brett, who, with her colleagues, has demonstrated that culture guides negotiators' strategic preferences, behaviors, and reactions to their counterparts' behaviors (Brett, Behfar, & Sanchez-Burks, 2014). In this chapter, we utilize Gunia, Brett, and Gelfand's (2016) input–process–outcome framework to organize our review and to understand cultural and situational inputs that influence key negotiation processes and outcomes. The input–process–outcome framework considers negotiations on the basis of the three parameters – inputs to the negotiation, the processes followed during the negotiation, and the outcomes of the negotiation. In addition, we delineate research that has focused on intercultural versus intracultural negotiations. Finally, we outline key cultural characteristics of negotiators that influence negotiation outcomes.

9.1   Cultural and Situational Inputs

We first discuss theoretical approaches to understanding how negotiators' psychological states are influenced by their cultures. Overall, although negotiators across different cultures may find themselves in similar situational contexts (e.g., being accountable to a constituent, negotiating in situations with power differentials), their culture causes them to respond to many of these contexts differently. Namely, there is variability in how these situational factors affect negotiation processes and outcomes for people from different cultures.

Cultural variations in negotiation styles have been described many centuries ago. For example, in 400 BC, the ancient Greek historian Herodotus, while observing cross-cultural negotiations, noted what he thought was the peculiar way in which Egyptians traded with the Greeks (Gelfand, Severance, & Fulmer, 2012; Herodotus, 2003). The vast majority of empirical negotiation research up to the late 20th century has been conducted in Western cultures, particularly in the United States (for a review, see Sycara, Gelfand, & Abbe, 2013). This focus on "Western, Educated, Industrialized, Rich, and Democratic" or WEIRD cultures (Henrich, Heine, & Norenzayan, 2010, p. 61) left a dearth of understanding of how individuals from different cultures negotiate. Moreover, this lack of research resulted in an implicit assumption that individuals around the world negotiate in a similar manner.

However, the 21st century witnessed the integration of culture and negotiations research by social psychologists and organizational behavior scholars, which has produced fruitful insights into how people from different cultures negotiate. Two theoretical perspectives have emerged outlining the rationale for why cultural differences emerge in negotiations: the cultural values perspective and the socio-ecological perspective.

9.1.1 Cultural Values Perspective

Much of the classic negotiations work draws from the *cultural values* perspective, in which researchers propose that differences in cultural values explain differences in individuals' negotiation behaviors. The cultural values perspective suggests that aspects of a culture shape individuals' cultural values and negotiation preferences. An assumption of this perspective is that "what the culture says is right and good becomes what people like" (Kim & Markus, 1999, p. 797). In other words, negotiators have little agency in their decisions and instead, behave in ways their culture tells them to behave.

The most popular measures to examine the effects of cultural values on negotiation have been Hui and Triandis' (1986) measure of individualism–collectivism, Hofstede's national cultural dimensions (1986), House's Global Leadership and Organizational Behavior Effectiveness (GLOBE) measure (House, Hanges, Javidan, Dorfman, & Gupta, 2004), and Schwartz's (2006) cultural value orientation measure. There are conceptual overlaps between these measures; for example, future orientation, power distance, and egalitarianism are key constructs within several of these measures.

Recent empirical work has established that cultural values influence negotiation processes and outcomes. For example, researchers have demonstrated that power distance is related with competitive negotiation styles, whereas uncertainty avoidance is associated with cooperative negotiation styles (Caputo, Ayoko, Amoo, & Menke, 2019). However, critics have said that the cultural values perspective does not adequately explain how cultural practices change over time (Morris, Hong, Chiu, & Liu, 2015), and does not sufficiently and reliably explain within-culture variations in negotiation practices (Caputo, Ayoko, Amoo, & Menke, 2019). Nevertheless, a substantial amount of research has continued to use this framework to examine cultural differences in negotiations.

9.1.2   Socio-ecological Perspective

An alternative theoretical perspective is the *socio-ecological perspective.* In contrast to the cultural values perspective, the socio-ecological perspective pays greater attention to how the situational context influences the human psychology. The socio-ecological perspective suggests that individuals' perceptions, attitudes, and behaviors are shaped in part by their larger societal context, including the social (e.g., economic, political, and religious) and natural (e.g., climate, geographical) habitat in which one is situated (Oishi & Graham, 2010). This perspective suggests that the selection of strategies by individuals is based on how rational and superior they perceive these strategies to be in a particular ecological context (Gelfand, Severance, & Fulmer, 2012; Yamagishi, Cook, & Watabe, 1998). This perspective therefore differs from the cultural values perspective: whereas the cultural values perspective suggests that individuals' behaviors emerge with little consideration of the behaviors' strategic value, the socio-ecological perspective suggests that individuals possess agency and will choose strategies that are culturally adaptive within their physical and social context.

While still a nascent area of work, recent research has utilized this perspective to study negotiations. One socio-ecological factor is the level of tightness or looseness of a culture (Gelfand, Raver, Nishii, Leslie, Lun, Lim, … Yamaguchi, 2011). Cultural tightness and looseness arise from a variety of ecological and historical factors (e.g., history of conflict, environmental threats; see Gelfand, Raver, Nishii, Leslie, Lun, Lim, ... Yamaguchi, 2011). Tighter cultures are those in which social norms are very clear and defined: when individuals deviate from these norms, they are punished. In contrast, in looser cultures, social norms are less collectively defined and sanctioning is used less often as a tool to reinforce norms. For instance, Gelfand, Gordon, Li, Choi, and Prokopowicz (2018) examined over 6,000 international merger and acquisition negotiations and found that the greater the differences between the two merging companies in terms of tightness–looseness, the longer the mergers took to negotiate and finalize.

Another socio-ecological factor that has received attention with regards to negotiations is the culture's level of relational mobility, or how much an individual's environment allows them to form and break relationships at will (Oishi, Schug, Yuki, & Axt, 2015). In relationally stable cultures, relationships between individuals tend to be more consistent, stable, and reliable. In relationally mobile cultures, relationships constantly shift and tend to be more transient. There is evidence that this cultural factor may also shape the psychology of negotiators across different cultures and influence their negotiation outcomes (Wang & Leung, 2010; Wang, Leung, See, & Gao, 2011).

In sum, the *socio-ecological perspective* provides a more dynamic perspective of culture than the *cultural values perspective* by suggesting that shifting socio-ecological factors may influence individuals' strategic options and choices within negotiations (Brett, Gunia, & Teucher, 2017). Moreover, because the assumptions of the cultural values perspective are that national borders define a culture, researchers often draw from the socio-ecological perspective to understand and explain differences in behavior within national borders. While empirical support has been more limited than the support for the cultural values perspective, the socio-ecological perspective allows for rich avenues of future research to explain the mixed cultural findings within the literature.

9.2 Intracultural and Intercultural Negotiations

One important delineation is whether individuals are negotiating intraculturally or interculturally. Intracultural negotiations refer to negotiations that occur between individuals of the same culture. Intercultural negotiations refer to negotiations that occur between individuals from different cultures.

Much of the research has focused on comparative intracultural negotiations – the comparison of intracultural negotiations between two or more cultures (e.g., comparing and contrasting the outcomes of an American–American dyad versus a Chinese–Chinese dyad; Brett, Gunia, & Teucher, 2017). Whereas the majority of literature has focused on comparative intracultural negotiations, there is a growing literature on intercultural negotiations. There are particular challenges with regards to intercultural negotiations because "the mental models of negotiators from one culture may not map on to the mental models of negotiators from another culture" (Brett, 2000, p. 97). For example, Liu, Friedman, Barry, Gelfand, and Zhang (2012) found that those negotiating intraculturally (an American–American dyad or a Chinese–Chinese dyad) are more likely to share an understanding of the situation than dyads negotiating interculturally (American–Chinese dyad). As a result, achieving joint gains is more difficult in intercultural settings than in intracultural settings because it is more challenging to build consensus around the key issues and negotiation points (Brett & Okumura, 1998).

However, it is important to recognize that the motivational states of the negotiator matter. Researchers have found that a motivation for a positive self-image resulted in more consensus in intercultural dyads than in intracultural dyads. This may be because individuals who possess a high concern for face are especially apprehensive about the social aspects unique to intercultural negotiations (e.g., how will my counterpart perceive my culture?). In contrast, a need for closure, a cognitive style in which individuals possess a desire for structure and closure, resulted in less consensus in intracultural dyads than in intercultural dyads because these individuals will be less open to engaging with the dissimilar mental models of the other-culture negotiator (Liu, Friedman, Barry, Gelfand, & Zhang, 2012; Liu, Friedman, & Hong, 2012).

As we continue to discuss the effects of culture on negotiation processes and outcomes, we specify when the research examines intracultural versus intercultural negotiations.

9.3   Negotiation Processes

An intriguing avenue researchers have taken is to understand how culture influences the negotiation process or the way individuals behave during negotiations. Adair and Brett (2004; 2005) contend that the way in which the stages of a negotiation unfold is a generally universal process. Negotiations can be likened to a "dance": first, negotiators relationally position themselves (e.g., "set the stage" and contend for power), then they focus on figuring out the problem (e.g., via information-gathering and exchange), next they propose solutions (e.g., by providing offers), and finally, they attempt to reach an agreement.

However, the characteristics of an individual's culture has unique implications for the type of negotiation strategies they choose. Namely, cultural researchers have compared decisions to employ distributive (value claiming) versus integrative (value creating) strategies during the negotiation process between cultures, and furthermore have examined how these strategies influence the outcomes of negotiations. We outline below how culture influences the information exchange and the communication patterns during the negotiation.

9.3.1   Information Exchange

Culture influences how individuals approach each of the negotiation stages and how they choose to exchange information during the negotiation (Adair & Brett, 2005). We highlight some of the most prominent areas of research, including what type of communication strategies negotiators use (question and answering versus substantiation and offers).

9.3.1.1   High and Low Context

Culture can influence the communication strategies negotiators choose. Specifically, whether a culture is low context (e.g., more direct) versus high context (e.g., more indirect; Hall, 1976) has been demonstrated to influence the negotiation process (Adair & Brett, 2004).

Low context cultures include a number of Western countries (e.g., U.S., Germany). The norms in low context cultures emphasize more direct and explicit information exchange, in which the messages provided by individuals are clearly stated in the words and messages used by negotiators.

Negotiators from low context cultures use question and answer (Q&A) strategies. Q&A strategies include negotiators asking questions about their counterparts' priorities and providing answers about their own priorities when asked.

On the other hand, some cultures (e.g., Hong Kong, Thailand, Russia) are high context and possess norms that emphasize implicit and indirect communication, in which the underlying meaning within words and messages is more understated and indirect. High context cultures tend to rely on substantiation and offer (S&O) strategies. Negotiators who use S&O strategies use offers to communicate their interests and emphasize certain types of information to signal their priorities and interests. These negotiators may also substantiate their offers by attempting to use publicly available information to persuade others. As such, when negotiating with a high context counterpart, negotiators must infer their counterparts' priorities and positions through indirect means.

In one comprehensive study, Adair and Brett (2004) examined both intracultural and intercultural negotiation dyads and found that the usage of S&O and Q&A sequences across time within the negotiation differed by culture. For example, researchers found that, as compared to low context or mixed context (one high, one low) dyads, high context dyads used more structural sequences of S&O in the beginning of the negotiation, however this difference in S&O sequences between cultural types diminished over time. Moreover, negotiators from high context cultures were more likely to respond more flexibly with their strategies. That is, high context dyads and mixed context dyads were more likely than low context dyads to use a combination of both Q&A and S&O strategies. This presumably occurred because low context negotiators find it difficult to interpret high context communication, and as a result, negotiators from high context cultures more easily adjust to the other negotiators' styles and utilize both types of strategies.

Research is somewhat mixed about the efficacy of these strategies in terms of negotiation performance. While research suggests that Q&A strategies are generally associated with higher joint gains and S&O strategies are generally associated with low joint gains, this is not always the case in all cultures (Brett, Gunia, & Teucher, 2017). Brett, Gunia, and Teucher (2017) proposed that one key characteristic that may explain this discrepancy is whether the negotiator possesses a holistic (i.e., consideration of the situation as a whole) versus an analytic (i.e., assigning aspects of the situation to specific categories) mindset. Specifically, negotiators who possess a holistic mindset might be better at securing joint gains when S&O strategies are used because they are able to infer priorities and interests within the offers that are being proposed.

9.3.1.2   High and Low Trust

Trust in negotiations is the willingness to be vulnerable to your counterparts based on the positive expectation that they will not take advantage of you (Kong, Dirks, & Ferrin, 2014). For example, a negotiator who trusts their counterpart will share information about their preferences, even if there is a risk that the counterpart might use that information to gain a distributive advantage. Research suggests that trust is positively associated with integrative (i.e., Q&A) strategies and higher joint outcomes and negatively associated with distributive (i.e., S&O) strategies and lower distributive outcomes (Kong, Dirks, & Ferrin, 2014).

Research has established that culture shapes the levels of trust within social exchange and negotiations (Yamagishi, Cook, & Watabe, 1998; Wang & Leung, 2010). In general, trust is low in Latin, Middle Eastern, and South Asian cultures, moderate in East Asian cultures, and high in Western cultures (Brett, Gunia, & Teucher, 2017). Culture influences how much negotiators trust their counterparts, with those from low trust cultures using S&O strategies and those from high trust cultures using Q&A strategies. These processes, in turn, may influence negotiation outcomes. For example, Gunia, Brett, Nandkeolyar, and Kamdar (2011) utilized a comparative intracultural negotiations paradigm and found that Indian dyads created lower joint gains than American dyads did because levels of trust and Q&A strategies were lower between Indian negotiators.

While typically, those from high trust cultures use Q&A strategies and low trust cultures use S&O strategies, there are distinct exceptions within certain cultures. Central and South American cultures, which are considered low trust cultures, show a more disparate set of strategies. For example, negotiators from Mexico and Spain rely more on S&O strategies, whereas negotiators from Brazil rely more on Q&A strategies. On the other hand, negotiators in East Asian cultures exhibit relatively high levels of trust, yet rely more on S&O strategies than on Q&A strategies. One explanation to explain this variation is that the effect of culturally based trust on the choice of strategy is moderated by levels of cultural tightness–looseness. Namely, the effect of low trust in Central and South American cultures on S&O strategies may be weaker because these cultures are loose. This cultural looseness affords individuals opportunities to deviate from S&O strategies and also utilize Q&A strategies (Brett, Gunia, & Teucher, 2017). In contrast, in East Asian cultures, high levels of trust may have less of an impact because cultural tightness focuses individuals on aspects of the situational norms. Because negotiation is viewed as a competitive task, negotiators in East Asian cultures may be less likely to use Q&A strategies than S&O strategies as doing so may pose a risk of them being taken advantage of.

9.3.2   Communication Styles

There is also some evidence that verbal and non-verbal communication during negotiations vary between cultures. Graham (1985) examined levels of silence and the number of interruptions of negotiators from the U.S., Brazil, and Japan. U.S. and Brazilian negotiators tended to avoid periods of silence as compared to Japanese negotiators. Moreover, Brazilian negotiators interrupted and said "no" significantly more than Japanese and American negotiators. Finally, individuals from these cultures differed in their levels of physical contact: Brazilian negotiators were more likely to touch each other than U.S. and Japanese negotiators.

9.3.3   Conflict Resolution Styles

Tinsley and Brett (2001) also demonstrated that cultural differences exist with respect to conflict resolution negotiation styles. They found that Americans and Germans used more interest-based strategies (e.g., suggesting tradeoffs, creating interest-based proposals) than Japanese individuals did during the negotiation. Moreover, they found that Japanese used more power-based strategies (e.g., making threats or rebuttals that highlight levels of power) than Germans, and that Germans used power-based strategies more than Americans did. Finally, they found that Germans used rights-based strategies more than Americans and Japanese did. They proposed that these effects occurred because of the congruence between the cultural values and the type of strategies used. For example, as egalitarian cultures value participatory decision making, individuals from those cultures (e.g., from the United States) will utilize interest-based strategies which allow all parties to provide input into the decision-making process.

9.4 Negotiation Outcomes

A substantial amount of work has focused on how culture shapes parties' distributive and integrative outcomes. In general, researchers have used a culture values framework to examine differences between national cultures. For example, Lugger, Geiger, Neun, and Backhaus (2015) found that in intracultural negotiations, German dyads created more value than Chinese dyads because German dyads utilized more integrative tactics during their negotiations (Lugger, Geiger, Neun, & Backhaus, 2015). Theoretically, Lugger, Geiger, Neun, & Backhaus (2015) drew their theory from House's GLOBE dimension of assertiveness (with China being a more assertive culture than Germany) to explain these differences. We outline the most prominent cultural characteristics used to explain the cultural differences in distributive and integrative outcomes: individualism/collectivism, egalitarianism/hierarchy, and emotions.

9.4.1 Individualism and Collectivism

Individualism focuses on the attainment of individual goals and collectivism emphasizes the attainment of group goals (Triandis, 2018). Negotiators from individualistic cultures have a preference for strategies that are more self-interested and help satisfy their own needs. In contrast, negotiators from collectivistic cultures are more inclined to utilize strategies that accommodate others and their concerns (Brett & Okumura, 1998; Holt & DeVore, 2005; Pearson & Stephan, 1998).

Research has shown that cultural differences in individualism and collectivism have implications for negotiation outcomes (see Toosi, Semnani-Azad, Shen, Mor, & Amanatullah, 2020, for a review). Brett and Okumura (1998) found that cultural differences in individualism and collectivism seemed to play a role in the level of joint gains. Intercultural negotiations between U.S. and Japanese dyads resulted in lower joint gains than intracultural U.S. dyads and Japanese dyads. This was likely because the different cultural schemas (individualistic versus collectivistic) of negotiators in intercultural negotiations interfered with the interaction between dyads and their ability to share information.

In addition to a direct effect on negotiation outcomes, cultural differences in individualism and collectivism also moderate the effects of certain aspects of the negotiators' situation and characteristics.

9.4.1.1   Accountability

Gelfand and Realo (1999) found that accountability to constituents (i.e., when one is an agent negotiating on behalf of another person) affects negotiators' psychological states and behaviors differentially, depending on one's levels of individualism and collectivism. For those who were low in collectivism, accountability increased levels of competitiveness and decreased joint outcomes. In contrast, for those high in collectivism, accountability increased levels of cooperativeness and increased joint gains. This presumably occurs because accountability heightens evaluative concerns, so individuals may feel compelled to act in ways that align with what is valued in their culture (competitiveness in individualistic cultures and cooperativeness in collectivistic cultures).

9.4.1.2   Gender

There also seems to be an interesting nuance in how individualism and collectivism of each culture shapes how gender influences the negotiation outcomes. Much of the research has been based in the United States, an individualistic culture, and has found that men are more likely to set more ambitious targets, initiate negotiations, and use more aggressive negotiation strategies (Babcock & Laschever, 2007). However, some research in collectivistic cultures, such as China and Peru, find the opposite. In China, women, as compared to men, are more likely to set more ambitious targets (Chen & Chen, 2012). Similarly, in Peru, female negotiators make more aggressive offers than male negotiators (Castillo, Petrie, Torero, & Vesterlund, 2013). These results have potential implications on economic performance in negotiations. Shan, Keller, and Joseph (2019) conducted a meta-analysis of negotiation behaviors from 30 national cultures. This meta-analysis found that men outperformed women in individualistic cultures, whereas women outperformed men in collectivistic cultures. The research suggests that gender norms are not universal. Rather, in individualistic cultures (e.g., the U.S.), competitive orientations (viewed as useful to achieve more in a negotiation) are considered a masculine trait, rather than a feminine trait. In contrast, in collectivistic cultures (e.g., China), competitive orientations are considered a feminine trait, rather than masculine trait (Shan, Keller, & Imai, 2016).

9.4.1.3   Communication Medium

Research suggests that, as compared to more U.S. negotiators, more collectivistic Hong Kong Chinese negotiators might use more distributive tactics instead of using integrative tactics in online formats. Rosette, Brett, Barsness, and Lytle (2012) examined intracultural negotiations and found that Hong Kong Chinese dyads negotiating via email were more likely to provide an opening offer and do distributively better than Hong Kong Chinese dyads negotiating face-to-face and U.S. dyads negotiating both via email and face-to-face. The authors posited that this occurred because email communication reduces the salience of social norms – in the case of Hong Kong, the collectivistic norm to be socially harmonious. As a result, email increases non-normative behaviors, such as the use of distributive tactics. Rosette, Brett, Barsness, and Lytle (2012) also examined intercultural negotiations and found a similar pattern of results. Hong Kong individuals negotiating online with U.S. individuals opened the negotiation with more aggressive offers. As a result, these opening offers anchored the negotiation and resulted in a distributive advantage by the Hong Kong individuals in the negotiation.

9.4.2   Egalitarianism and Hierarchy

Culture influences whether individuals prefer hierarchical relationships (i.e., a preference for differences in social status) or egalitarian relationships (i.e., a preference for equality). In negotiations, this preference has implications for perceptions of power (Brett & Okumura, 1998). Specifically, negotiators in egalitarian national cultures (i.e., the U.S.) were more likely to view that possessing a BATNA was an important source of power than those from hierarchical national cultures (i.e., Japan). Brett and Okumura (1998) theorized that this perceptual difference in perceptions of power plays a role in why intercultural negotiations were less likely to result in joint gains than intracultural negotiations.

Beyond national cultures, organizational cultures can also differ in terms of hierarchy and egalitarianism. In a line of work by Curhan and colleagues (2008), negotiation dyads were placed in a scenario in which the company possessed either an egalitarian or hierarchical culture. The authors posited that those in the egalitarian culture condition may be more focused than those in the hierarchical cultural condition on yielding to the other side, at the expense of value creation (which needs a balance of cooperation and competition). As compared to negotiation pairs who were placed in the hierarchical culture condition, negotiation pairs who were in the egalitarian culture condition achieved lower joint gains, but were more satisfied with the relationship.

9.4.3 Mood and Emotions

As outlined in Chapter 5, emotions can significantly influence negotiation processes and outcomes. While the majority of emotions research still generally focuses on North American and Western European populations, there is a growing area of work examining cultural patterns of emotions, and how they influence negotiations and bargaining. For example, cultural differences in individualism and collectivism, hierarchy and egalitarianism, and promotion and prevention focus, have been hypothesized to shape individuals' levels of positive and negative affect and emotions (Matsumoto, Yoo, & Nakagawa, 2008; Deng, Wang, Aime, Wang, Sivanathan, & Kim, 2021). In turn, affect and emotions influence how negotiators process information, interpret their negotiation partner's emotions and behaviors, and choose to respond and behave (George, Jones, & Gonzalez, 1998).

To date, the majority of research examining culture and emotions has focused on displays and reactions to anger within negotiations. There has been some work examining cultural differences in general levels of positive and negative affect and its effect on bargaining behavior.

9.4.3.1 Anger

Culture influences which displays of emotions are seen as appropriate and normative. As compared to Western cultures, the greater emphasis of interdependence and harmony in collectivistic cultures, such as East Asian cultures, means that displays of anger, an emotion that is incongruent with the idea of harmony, will be viewed as relatively inappropriate. As a result, displays of anger may result in more negative reactions in East Asian cultures, but more positive reactions in Western cultures.

Based on this theorizing, researchers have examined how expressions of anger in negotiations influence concession-making behavior in negotiations (Adam, Shirako, & Maddux, 2010). For individuals of European ethnicity, expressions of anger by their counterparts, as compared to lack of expressions of anger by their counterparts, were associated with these individuals of European ethnicity making larger concessions during the negotiation. For individuals of East Asian ethnicity, the reverse was true: expressions of anger by their counterparts, as compared to no expressions of anger by their counterparts, were associated with these East Asian individuals making smaller concessions during the negotiation.

Adam and Shirako (2013) hypothesized that the culture of the angry expresser would influence negotiation outcomes as well. In line with the concept of social harmony above, one stereotype is that European Americans are more emotionally expressive than are East Asians. As a result, the expression of non-stereotypic emotions, such as East Asian negotiators expressing anger, may engender stronger reactions by counterparts because these negotiators are viewed as more aggressive and threatening. In other words, an angry East Asian negotiator is perceived as tougher or more threatening as compared to an angry European American. In line with their theorizing, the researchers found that individuals were more likely to cooperate with angry East Asian negotiators as compared to angry European American negotiators because of increased perceptions of toughness.

9.4.3.2 Positive and Negative Emotions

While the majority of research has focused on anger, some work has also compared how positive and negative emotions differ between cultures and how these cultural differences influence outcomes within a bargaining context.

For example, Kopelman and Rosette (2008) examined reactions to positive (e.g., friendly, considerate) and negative (e.g., annoyed, angry) emotional displays. They found that East Asian negotiators, as compared to Israeli negotiators, were more likely to reject an ultimatum offer when their counterpart displayed negative rather than positive emotions. The researchers hypothesized that this occurred because negative emotions were seen as incongruent with the cultural values of social harmony in East Asian cultures.

Cultural signatures in positive and negative emotions not only influence one-shot interactions in bargaining contexts, but also influence positive versus negative behaviors over time. For example, Deng and colleagues (2021) demonstrated that, in a repeated, positively framed (i.e., giving) dictator game, Americans escalated positive behaviors (e.g., how much they gave to the other side increased over time) because they felt more happiness. However, in a repeated, negatively framed (i.e., taking) dictator game, Americans escalated negative behaviors (e.g., how much they took from the other side increased over time) because they felt more anxiety. The authors found that this occurred due to cultural differences in regulatory focus (promotion versus prevention focus) that were associated with specific emotions (i.e., anxiety and happiness), which then escalated giving or taking over time.

9.4.4   Negotiator Characteristics

Researchers have begun to examine whether certain characteristics of the negotiator will improve negotiation outcomes: cultural intelligence and cultural perspective-taking.

9.4.4.1   *Cultural Intelligence*

Cultural intelligence, also known as CQ, is an individual's ability to adapt to new cultural settings (Earley & Ang, 2003). This measure consists of four components: a cultural awareness of one's own and other's thoughts; an understanding of the other group's cultural values, beliefs, and norms; a motivation to learn about cultural differences; and an ability to behave in ways that are appropriate when interacting with people from different cultures. Researchers have established that CQ can influence negotiation processes and outcomes (Caputo, Ayoko, Amoo, & Menke, 2019; Groves, Feverherm, & Gu, 2015). For example, Imai and Gelfand (2010) found that high CQ individuals expressed a greater desire to cooperate than low CQ individuals. Moreover, as compared to negotiation dyads who were low in CQ, negotiation dyads who were high in CQ were more likely to engage integrative behaviors (e.g., information sharing) during the negotiation that resulted in greater joint outcomes. This occurred even when controlling for other types of intelligence (i.e., IQ and emotional intelligence), multi-cultural experiences, and personality factors (i.e., openness and extraversion). Other researchers have also found similar effects of CQ on negotiation processes.

9.4.4.2   *Cultural Perspective-Taking*

The act of perspective-taking, in which one imagines the world from another person's perspective (Galinsky, Ku, & Wang, 2005; Ku, Wang, & Galinsky, 2015), has been shown to help in both value claiming and creation. Drawing from this literature, Lee, Adair, and Seo (2013) introduced the concept of cultural perspective-taking, or the active consideration of another negotiation party's cultural norms, prior to the negotiation. In their empirical study, individuals of North American and East Asian descent took part in a simulated buyer–seller negotiation. Individuals who engaged in cultural perspective-taking claimed more value in the negotiation than those who engaged in non-cultural perspective-taking, presumably because those in the cultural perspective-taking condition were able to better anticipate the other parties' culturally driven behaviors.

9.5   Summary

This chapter provided an overview of how culture, a shared set of values, beliefs, norms, and behaviors, plays an important role in negotiations. We outlined the research on culture and negotiations using Gunia, Brett and Gelfand's (2016) input–process–outcome framework. First, we described the inputs that impact a negotiation by considering two theoretical perspectives: the cultural values perspective and the socio-ecological perspective. We also differentiated research that focuses on intercultural versus intracultural negotiations. Second, we considered the cultural strategies typically used during negotiations – specifically, we outlined how culture can influence the types of information exchange and the communication patterns seen in negotiations. Third, we outlined how culture influences distributive and integrative outcomes in negotiations. We wrapped up this chapter by considering the key cultural characteristics of negotiators that influence negotiation outcomes.

10   Communication media

The ways negotiators communicate has shifted and evolved over time. In the late 1960s, negotiation researchers started to examine this topic and consider the effects of different communication media. For example, researchers have compared and contrasted negotiations that take place face-to-face versus telephone (Morley & Stephenson, 1969) versus written messages (Smith, 1969). Since this early research, a greater variety of communication media has emerged with the advent of computer-mediated communication (CMC) formats such as email, text messaging, and video platforms. Understanding the effects of communication media on negotiations has become an area of research with growing relevance as deal-making now often crosses geographic borders and because of events such as the COVID-19 pandemic that have made it challenging to negotiate in person.

Notably, researchers have introduced several theoretical frameworks which outline how and why different communication media influence negotiation outcomes. Below, we draw from several crucial reviews and meta-analyses (e.g., Stuhlmacher & Citera, 2005; Geiger, 2020) to provide an overview of the different theoretical perspectives that have emerged in this area. Whereas earlier frameworks suggested that communication media that allow for the greater exchange of visual- and audio-based cues improve negotiation processes and outcomes, newer frameworks have proposed the importance of considering key factors that moderate the effects of communication media on negotiation outcomes. For example, some studies have demonstrated that negotiating face-to-face as compared to via telephone or written text improves outcomes (Valley, Moag, & Bazerman, 1998), while other studies have established that face-to-face negotiators perform worse than negotiators using other communication media (Carnevale, Pruitt, & Seilheimer, 1981).

10.1   Media Richness Theory

A classic approach to understanding the effects of communication media is highlighted in Media Richness Theory. This theory was first introduced in the communication literature by organizational behavior scholars Richard Daft and Robert Lengel. Daft and Lengel (1983) outlined five types of communication media: face-to-face, telephone, personal written correspondence, formal written correspondence, and formal numeric correspondence (i.e., using numbers to communicate). The authors noted that these types of media vary with regards to four specific characteristics: the speed of feedback (i.e., synchronous versus asynchronous), the channel of communication (i.e., visual versus audio), the source of communication (e.g., personal versus impersonal), and the language used (i.e., body, spoken, and numeric).

Media Richness Theory suggests that certain media can carry more information, better transmit information, and allow for more effective communication (Daft & Lengel, 1986). For example, face-to-face communication is considered to be the richest medium of communication, as the feedback is immediate, it involves both visual and audio channels, is more personal, and includes both body language and spoken language. As related to negotiations, researchers have argued that richer communications channels in which you are able to see, hear, and quickly respond to counterparts will result in improved negotiation outcomes because it engenders better information exchange and greater trust and rapport. In line with this theorizing, research has found that media richness influences levels of cooperation, information exchange, and negotiation outcomes. We outline some key findings below.

10.1.1   Cooperation

Richer communication media have been thought to increase levels of cooperation (Purdy, Nye, & Balakrishnan, 2000). For example, empirical research has established that negotiators who are able speak to and hear their counterparts were more likely to use cooperative tactics (Smith, 1969; Sheffield, 1995; Purdy, Nye, & Balakrishnan, 2000). The authors speculated that this occurred because audio communication media allow negotiators to better understand their counterparts' interests. Audio communication allows for greater emotional interpretation and accuracy – specifically, the pitch, loudness, and speed of voices – which help individuals better read the emotional tenor of the conversation and respond based on these emotional cues, thereby improving cooperation (Daft & Lengel, 1986).

Other research has also found that richer communication media facilitate more cooperation and better negotiation outcomes. Purdy, Nye, and Balakrishnan (2000) compared and contrasted face-to-face, video, telephone, and CMC, and examined how these media influenced negotiation processes, outcomes, and downstream subjective outcomes (i.e., outcome satisfaction and desire to negotiate together in the future). In particular, the authors proposed that media richness was positively associated with collaborative and cooperative bargaining approaches during the negotiation, which would in turn increase negotiation efficiency (i.e., finishing the negotiation more quickly), joint outcomes, and subjective outcomes. Indeed, the authors found that negotiators using richer communication media reached agreements more quickly because the negotiators were more cooperative during the negotiation. Moreover, richer communication media resulted in greater outcome satisfaction and an increased desire to negotiate with the same counterpart in the future.

A meta-analysis by Stuhlmacher and Citera (2005) compared face-to-face negotiations to CMC negotiations (e.g., email/text, video-conferencing). The authors found that negotiators expressed less hostility and achieved greater joint profit when they were in face-to-face negotiations as compared to CMC negotiations. There is also evidence that face-to-face negotiations result in more equal outcomes between negotiators, whereas written negotiations resulted in the greatest amount of impasses (Valley, Moag, & Bazerman, 1998). This is thought to occur because, as compared to written negotiations, face-to-face negotiations increase levels of empathy, which then result in a desire to fulfill the needs of one's counterpart(s) (Roth, 1995). Similarly, Turnbull, Strickland, and Shaver (1976) found that individuals negotiating face-to-face achieved better negotiation outcomes than those using audio-visual platforms and audio-only platforms. The authors suggested that these patterns of results might have occurred because negotiators were more responsive to their counterparts' needs when media richness was higher.

10.1.2 Information Exchange

The speed of feedback can also influence information exchange. When negotiators cannot respond to each other right away (i.e., in asynchronous media such as email), they cannot as easily evaluate each other's opinions. As a result, asynchronous communication channels make it harder for negotiators to exchange information and easier for misinterpretations to arise (Friedman & Currall, 2003).

Also, when comparing different forms of CMC, individuals who negotiated using audio and visual channels were better able to exchange information and come to a mutual understanding over negotiation facts than individuals who could only communicate via text (Yuan, Head, & Du, 2003). Similarly, face-to-face interaction has also been found to improve coordination in bargaining games because it allows for multiple ways for the information to be received (Brosig, Ockenfels, & Weimann, 1999; McGinn, Thompson, & Bazerman, 2003).

10.1.3 Deception

In line with Media Richness Theory, Valley, Moag, and Bazerman (1998) found that sellers in a simulated negotiation were less likely to lie in face-to-face negotiations than in telephone negotiations or written negotiations. In turn, reduced deception led to increased joint outcomes in the negotiation. One reason for why there is less deception in face-to-face contexts is that negotiators are better able to accurately detect deception and emotional content in face-to-face contexts than in electronic written formats (Giordano, Stoner, Brouer, & George, 2007; Laubert & Parlamis, 2019).

10.2 Communication Grounding Theory

Negotiation researchers have drawn from Clark and Brennan's (1991) Communication Grounding Theory, which proposes that there are certain communication tools that allow for individuals interacting to achieve grounding, a shared understanding or cognition about the interpersonal situation and dynamics. Face-to-face conversations allow for greater grounding than other communication media such as email because of co-presence (participants have a shared surrounding and can visualize what others are seeing), visibility (they can see each other's expressions), audibility (they can hear each other), co-temporality (each party can hear things at the same time), simultaneity (they can simultaneously send and receive communication), and sequentiality (the conversation goes in a certain order).

Researchers have suggested that because it is less able to create a shared understanding, email communication (versus face-to-face) may escalate conflict during disputes (Friedman & Currall, 2003), and pure text-based communications (versus text in combination with other media) will reduce communication efficiency (Yuan, Head, & Du, 2003). Similarly, Geiger (2014) drew from communication grounding theory and determined that negotiators achieved better outcomes and were more satisfied with the outcome when communicating face-to-face than via text. Johnson and Cooper (2009) found that as compared to face-to-face negotiations, telephone negotiations reduced emotional communication and concession-making, which then reduced the likelihood of agreement.

10.3   The Barrier Effect

Media Richness Theory and Communication Grounding Theory both suggest that communication channels that allow for more social cues will consistently improve negotiation processes and outcomes. However, empirical findings suggest that this is not the case and that, at times, other communication channels produce better outcomes (Citera, Beauregard, & Mitsuya, 2005; Lewis & Fry, 1977). For example, Lewis and Fry (1977) demonstrated that when peoples' individualistic orientations were heightened (i.e., when they were told to disregard their counterparts' needs and focus on their own needs), negotiators who could hear, but could not see, their counterparts, outperformed those who could both see and hear their counterparts. In another study, negotiators who could send text messages synchronously versus asynchronously acted more contentiously, exhibited greater negative emotions, and exchanged less negotiation information (Pesendorfer & Koeszegi, 2006).

A theory called the Barrier Effect has been used to explain these situations. This theory proposes that the ability to visually observe the other side will increase competitiveness during negotiations (Pruitt, 1981). Indeed, there is some empirical evidence that negotiators who can see the other side (versus those who cannot) were more hostile, and as a result, less integrative outcomes were reached (Carnevale & Isen, 1986; Carnevale, Pruitt, & Seilheimer, 1981; Lewis & Fry, 1977).

While Media Richness Theory and Communication Grounding Theory suggest that richer communication media such as face-to-face improves negotiation processes and outcomes, the Barrier Effect proposes that these communication media will actually harm processes and outcomes. Because there has been empirical support for all of these frameworks, newer theoretical frameworks have considered when and why richer communication media are harmful versus helpful. These theoretical frameworks have included Social Information Processing Theory and Communication Orientation Theory.

10.4   Social Information Processing Theory

Social Information Processing Theory provides the perspective that richer communication media may be less impactful once interpersonal connections are established between communicators (Walther, 1992; 1994). In other words, whereas it is more difficult to initially establish negotiation rapport in less-rich communication media, over time, negotiators will be able to build meaningful rapport regardless of communication medium.

Social Information Processing Theory also predicts that, in certain ways, less-rich communication channels may actually be better at establishing rapport than more-rich communication channels. For example, less-rich channels are convenient and easily available and thus can provide interpersonal connections that would be more difficult to establish using richer channels. Empirical research has found support for this theory. For example, Croson (1999) demonstrated that when negotiators were given ample time to negotiate (i.e., two weeks), joint outcomes were marginally higher when individuals negotiated via email than via face-to-face. Similarly, McGinn and Keros (2002) found that in telephone and email negotiations, possessing a close relationship between negotiators enhanced cooperation, increased the likelihood of issue tradeoffs, and resulted in more equal payoffs. However, the effects of a close relationship were weaker in face-to-face negotiations (McGinn & Keros, 2002). In sum, this theoretical perspective suggests that the temporal and relational dynamics of the negotiation context can dramatically alter the effects of communication medium on negotiation outcomes and processes.

10.5 Communication Orientation Theory

Another recent theoretical perspective is the Communication Orientation Theory, developed by Swaab, Galinsky, Medvec, and Diermeier (2012). Similar to Social Information Processing Theory, Communication Orientation Theory predicts that the effects of media richness on negotiation processes and outcomes will depend on the type of relationship negotiators possess. However, the Communication Orientation Theory attempts to more explicitly outline when and why certain communication media will be beneficial, neutral, or harmful. Specifically, this theory suggests that increased communication media with richness, in the form of greater visual, vocal, and synchronous information during communication, has differential effects based on the type of interpersonal orientation negotiators possess. The authors broke down the individual orientations into neutral, cooperative, or competitive, and performed a meta-analysis that confirmed their predictions.

10.5.1 Neutral Orientations

The authors predicted and found that media richness positively affects negotiators with neutral orientations, that is, those that do not have pre-existing cooperative or competitive orientations. Face-to-face interactions are usually assumed to be cooperative in nature because it is socially desirable to do so – as such, the assumption going into face-to-face conversations is that people will be willing to share information during conversations and that people will act with integrity (Krauss & Chiu, 1998). In line with this theorizing, the authors argue that this occurs because richer communication channels can provide social cues that enhance rapport and trust. For example, when negotiators are able to see their counterparts, they are able to feel that they are being accepted when their counterparts smile or nod their heads. Similarly, audio communication can have similar benefits because counterparts' immediate verbal affirmations provide instantiations of affirmation. As a result, this may increase the tendency for negotiators to exchange information (Thompson & Nadler, 2002).

10.5.2 Cooperative Orientations

Swaab, Galinsky, Medvec, and Diermeier (2012) also predicted and found that communication media was less relevant to negotiators with cooperative orientations. When individuals negotiate over time, they develop competitive or cooperative reputations that shape their orientations toward their counterparts. Negotiators who possess a more cooperative communication orientation will be concerned with not only their own, but also their counterparts' welfare. Because individuals with cooperative orientations are likely to have interacted in the past in a positive manner, they possess higher levels of trust and rapport and are more willing to share and exchange information, such as what their issue priorities are, during the negotiation (DeDreu, Weingart, & Kwon, 2000). As a result, the communication medium may have less of an impact on negotiators with cooperative orientations.

10.5.3 Competitive Orientations

Finally, Swaab and colleagues (2012) predicted that richer communication media would negatively impact outcomes of negotiators with competitive orientations. When negotiators view their counterparts in a competitive manner, they may attempt to protect their interests by using competitive tactics themselves (White, Tynan, Galinsky, & Thompson, 2004). This protective behavior can be intensified in negotiations that take place in richer communication media, as the salience of the competitive tactics become heightened. For example, synchronous negotiations in which negotiators can see unhappy expressions and hear the raised voices of their counterparts likely intensify negative emotions. In turn, these negative cues may decrease the likelihood of information exchange that would improve tradeoff possibilities between negotiators (Pruitt & Carnevale, 1993).

The concept of shuttle diplomacy has been successfully used to manage the competitive situations in which negotiation parties possess little trust, and direct communication only exacerbates an already negative situation. Shuttle diplomacy is when two parties in a dispute do not negotiate directly. Instead, a third party sends messages back and forth between the two parties. This lack of synchronicity and not being able to see the other side's negative emotions and statements allows for the possibility that better information will be exchanged. One well-known example of shuttle diplomacy was when the United States President Jimmy Carter passed messages and proposals between hostile Egyptian and Israeli leaders. As a result, these two parties eventually were able to sign a treaty (Hoffman, 2011).

In summary, the meta-analysis by Swaab and colleagues (2012) found support for Media Richness Theory by establishing a main effect for communication richness – negotiators who were able to see, hear, and respond immediately exhibited greater overall negotiation outcomes. Moreover, in line with Communication Orientation Theory, the effect of communication medium on negotiation outcomes was moderated by negotiator orientation: the overall presence of the aforementioned channels increased negotiation outcomes for neutral-oriented negotiators, did not influence cooperatively oriented negotiators, and decreased outcomes for competitively oriented negotiators. When these communication media were examined separately, the effects were replicated.

10.6 Additional Moderators

In addition to the aforementioned research, other research shows that the effect of communication media on negotiation outcomes depends on characteristics of the negotiator and negotiation, and also the social context in which the negotiation is situated.

10.6.1 Negotiator Characteristics

10.6.1.1 Gender

A meta-analysis by Stuhlmacher and her colleagues (2007) examined the moderating role of gender. They theorized that as compared to virtual negotiations, face-to-face negotiations possess a stronger set of expectations for social interaction that are established and increase the salience of negotiators' gender roles that guide their behavior. As a result, women negotiators may be less hostile in face-to-face negotiations than in virtual negotiations because acting aggressively is inconsistent with the gender stereotypes of women. Because the salience of negotiators' gender roles is weakened in virtual negotiations, women may act less in line with gender stereotypes and act more in line with the stereotypic expectations of negotiators (i.e., acting assertively to get what they want). Indeed, the meta-analysis of 43 negotiation studies found support for this effect. Moreover, the meta-analysis also demonstrated that communication medium did not influence levels of hostility for men because regardless of the medium, assertive behavior aligns with both men's gender expectations and negotiator expectations.

10.6.1.2 Personality Type

Researchers have examined how negotiators' personality types (see Chapter 7 for full discussion of individual differences) moderate the relationship between communication medium and negotiation outcomes. Much of the work has focused on understanding the effects of the Dark Triad (psychopathy, Machiavellianism, and narcissism). Psychopathy is characterized by abnormal social behavior and lack of empathy, Machiavellianism is characterized by a desire for personal gain through deception and manipulation, and narcissism involves extreme egocentrism and an excessive need for attention.

Crossley, Woodworth, Black, and Hare (2016) examined how the combination of communication medium and the negotiator's dark triad personality characteristics influences negotiation outcomes. They found that face-to-face negotiations resulted in better individual (i.e., distributive) outcomes than CMC negotiations (in the form of online chat negotiations) for those who reported possessing high levels of the dark triad traits. In contrast, for those reporting that they possessed low levels of the dark triad traits, CMC negotiations led to better individual outcomes than face-to-face negotiations. The authors theorized that this occurred because in face-to-face negotiations, individuals who possess dark triad traits, who focus on exploiting and manipulating others for self-gain, may be more persuasive in convincing others to let them get what they want. However, in online negotiations, their manipulative tactics may be seen as more hostile. For example, the authors coded the online language of psychopaths and it was assessed to be less comprehensible and more aggressive.

Another study by Fry (1985) examined the joint effects of communication medium and Machiavellianism on joint outcomes. In this study, individuals were either assigned to a condition in which they negotiated with both visual and audio cues or to a condition in which they negotiated with just audio cues, with a physical barrier between them so they could not see the other person. Fry found that mixed-Machiavellianism negotiation dyads (one participant with high levels and one with low) negotiating with both visual and audio contact performed worse than those negotiating without visual contact. However, communication medium didn't seem to influence dyads in which both participants were low in Machiavellianism or dyads in which both participants were high in Machiavellianism. The authors suggested that communication medium only influenced mixed-Machiavellianism dyads because the low Machiavellian negotiator felt greater apprehension when interacting with the high Machiavellian negotiator when there were visual cues, and as a result, was less able to generate feasible offers that helped the dyad achieve higher joint outcomes.

10.6.2 Negotiation Characteristics

10.6.2.1 Negotiation Rationale

One finding is that communication medium may moderate the effects of the type of rationales used by negotiators on value claiming (distributive outcomes). The authors found that negotiators who prepared in-depth rationales (versus simple rationales) to substantiate their positions were able to claim more value when the online communication was synchronous (i.e., instant messaging). However, the type of rationale did not influence value claiming when the online communication was asynchronous (i.e., email). The authors proposed that this occurred because during synchronous negotiations, the negotiators who had prepared in-depth arguments were more likely to bluff and draw concessions from counterparts than negotiators who had prepared more simple arguments. However, in asynchronous negotiations, this mediation was less likely to occur.

10.6.3 Social Context

10.6.3.1 Culture

Swaab and colleagues (2012) also explored whether cultural context moderated the effects of communication medium. The authors broke down the studies in their meta-analysis into Eastern cultures (e.g., East Asia and the Middle East) and Western cultures (e.g., the United States and Western Europe) and drew from the interdependence and independence literature to make their predictions. They posited that because individuals from interdependent cultures derive positive feelings about themselves from developing and maintaining close relationships with others (Cross, Bacon, & Morris, 2000), they may be more cooperatively oriented. In contrast, those from independent cultures tend to gain positive emotions from highlighting their unique selves and may be more competitively oriented. As a result, communication medium may be more impactful for those from independent cultures than interdependent cultures, as negotiators in interdependent cultures may be more likely to act cooperatively (e.g., share and exchange information during the negotiation) regardless of communication medium. Indeed, results of the meta-analysis established that communication medium (specifically, visual and vocal channels; there were not enough studies to test for the effects of synchronous channels) had less of an impact in interdependent cultures than in independent cultures.

10.6.3.2 Type of Relationship

In line with these findings, while Stuhlmacher and Citera (2005) found in their meta-analysis that negotiators interacting virtually exhibit more hostility and achieve lower outcomes than face-to-face negotiators, they also found that these effects were further influenced by the nature of the relationship between negotiators. Specifically, these effects were exacerbated when negotiators were strangers (i.e., they had not had a previous interaction). In another finding, the negative effects of virtual negotiations were mitigated when negotiators expected to interact in the future. These results suggest that relationship characteristics that increase feelings of psychological distance between negotiators will only further widen the relational gap that virtual communication channels bring.

10.7 Summary

In this chapter, we outlined the literature on negotiations and communication medium and provided an overview on the different theoretical frameworks. We started with Media Richness Theory and Communication Grounding Theory, which both suggest that communication channels that better transmit information and allow for grounding will improve negotiation processes and outcomes. We then described research supporting the Barrier Effect, which proposes that greater communication richness will increase competitiveness and hostility during negotiations. We then described findings supporting Social Information Processing Theory and Communication Orientation Theory, which suggests that the relational dynamics of the negotiation context can dramatically alter the effects of communication medium on negotiation outcomes and processes. Finally, we outlined additional findings that the effect of communication medium depends on characteristics of the negotiator and negotiation, and also the social context in which the negotiation is situated.

References

Aaldering, H., Zerres, A., & Steinel, W. (2020). Constituency norms facilitate unethical negotiation behavior through moral disengagement. *Group Decision and Negotiation, 29*(5), 969-991.

Adair, W. L., & Brett, J. M. (2004). Culture and negotiation processes. In M. J. Gelfand, & J. M. Brett (Eds.), *The handbook of negotiation and culture* (pp. 158-176). Stanford, CA: Stanford University Press.

Adair, W. L., & Brett, J. M. (2005). The negotiation dance: Time, culture, and behavioral sequences in negotiation. *Organizational Science, 16*(1), 33-51.

Adam, H., & Brett, J. M. (2015, November). Context matters: The social effects of anger in cooperative, balanced, and competitive negotiation situations. *Journal of Experimental Social Psychology, 61*, 44-58.

Adam, H., & Shirako, A. (2013). Not all anger is created equal: The impact of the expresser's culture on the social effects of anger in negotiations. *Journal of Applied Psychology, 98*(5), 785-798.

Adam, H., Shirako, A., & Maddux, W. W. (2010). Cultural variance in the interpersonal effects of anger in negotiations. *Psychological Science, 21*(6), 882-889.

Adler, R. S. (2007). Negotiating with liars. *MIT Sloan Management Review, 48*, 69-74.

Allais, M. (1953). Le comportement de l'homme rationnel devant le risque: Critique des postulate et aximes de l'ecole Americaine. *Econometrica, 21*(4), 503-546. doi:doi:10.2307/1907921

Allred, K. G., Mallozzi, J. S., Matsui, F., & Faia, C. P. (1997). The influence of anger and compassion on negotiation performance. *Organizational Behavior and Human Decision Processes, 70*(3), 175-187.

Amanatullah, E. T., & Morris, M. W. (2010). Negotiating gender roles: Gender differences in assertive negotiating are mediated by women's fear of backlash and attenuated when negotiating on behalf of others. *Journal of Personality and Social Psychology, 98*(2), 256-267.

Amanatullah, E. T., & Tinsley, C. H. (2013). Punishing female negotiators for asserting too much…or not enough: Exploring why advocacy moderates backlash against assertive female negotiators. *Organizational Behavior and Human Decision Processes, 120*(1), 110-122.

Amanatullah, E. T., Morris, M. W., & Curhan, J. R. (2008). Negotiators who give too much: Unmitigated communion, relational anxieties, and economic costs in distributive and integrative bargaining. *Journal of Personality and Social Psychology, 95*(3), 723-738.

Ames, D. R. (2008). Assertiveness expectancies: How hard people push depends on the consequences they predict. *Journal of Personality and Social Psychology*, 95(6), 1541-1557.

Ames, D. R., & Mason, M. F. (2015). Tandem anchoring: Informational and politeness effects of range offers in social exchange. *Journal of Personality and Social Psychology*, 108(2), 254-274.

Anderson, C., & Shirako, A. (2008). Are individuals' reputations related to their history of behavior? *Journal of Personality and Social Psychology*, 94(2), 320-333.

Anderson, C., & Thompson, L. L. (2004, November). Affect from the top down: How powerful individuals' positive affect shapes negotiations. *Organizational Behavior and Human Decision Processes*, 95(2), 125-139.

Appelt, K. C., & Higgins, E. T. (2010). My way: How strategic preferences vary by negotiator role and regulatory focus. *Journal of Experimental Social Psychology*, 46(6), 1138-1142.

Applbaum, A. (1996). Rules of the game, permissible harms, and the principle of fair play. In R. I. Zeckhauser, R. L. Keeney, & J. K. Sebenius (Eds.), Wise choices: *Decisions, games, and negotiations* (pp. 301-321). Boston, MA: Harvard Business School Press.

Aquino, K. (1998). The effects of ethical climate and the availability of alternatives on the use of deception during negotiation. *International Journal of Conflict Management*, 9, 195-217.

Aquino, K., Freeman, D., Reed II, A., Lim, V. K., & Felps, W. (2009). Testing a social-cognitive model of moral behavior: The interactive influence of situations and moral identity centrality. *Journal of Personality and Social Psychology*, 97(1), 123-141.

Argyle, M., & Henderson, M. (1985). The rules of relationships. In S. Duck, & D. Perlman (Eds.), *Understanding personal relationships: An interdisciplinary approach* (pp. 63-84). London: Sage Publications.

Arriaga, X. B., & Rusbult, C. E. (1998). Standing in my partner's shoes: Partner perspective taking and reactions to accommodative dilemmas. *Personality and Social Psychology Bulletin*, 24(9), 927-948.

Aykac, T., Wilken, R., Jacob, F., & Prime, N. (2017). Why teams achieve higher negotiation profits than individuals: The mediating role of deceptive tactics. *Journal of Business and Industrial Marketing; Santa Barbara*, 32(4), 567-579.

Babcock, L., & Laschever, S. (2007). *Women don't ask: The high cost of avoiding negotiation – and positive strategies for change*. London: Bantam Press.

Babcock, L., & Laschever, S. (2009). *Women don't ask*. Princeton, NJ: Princeton University Press.

Babcock, L., Gelfand, M., Small, D., & Stayn, H. (2006). Gender differences in the propensity to initiate negotiations. In D. De Cremer, M. Zeelenberg, & J. K. Murnighan (Eds.), *Social psychology and economics* (pp. 239-259). Mahwah, NJ: Lawrence Erlbaum Associates Publishers.

Barroso, A., & Brown, A. (2021). Gender pay gap in US held steady in 2020. *Pew Research Center*.

Barry, B., & Friedman, R. A. (1998). Bargainer characteristics in distributive and integrative negotiation. *Journal of Personality and Social Psychology*, 74(2), 345-359.

Barry, B., & Oliver, R. L. (1996). Affect in dyadic negotiation: A model and propositions. *Organizational Behavior and Human Decision Processes, 67,* 127-143.

Bazerman, M. H., & Gillespie, J. J. (1999, September–October). Betting on the future: The virtues of contingent contracts. *Harvard Business Review, 77*(5), 155-160.

Bazerman, M. H., Loewenstein, G. F., & White, S. H. (1992). Reversals of preference in allocation decisions: Judging an alternative versus choosing among alternatives. *Administrative Science Quarterly, 37*(2), 220–240.

Bazerman, M. H., & Neale, M. A. (1982, October). Improving negotiation effectiveness under final offer arbitration: The role of selection and training. *Journal of Applied Psychology, 67*(5), 543-548.

Bazerman, M. H., & Neale, M. A. (1992). *Negotiating rationally.* New York: Free Press.

Bazerman, M. H., Loewenstein, G. F., & White, S. H. (1992). Reversals of preference in allocation decisions: Judging an alternative versus choosing among alternatives. *Administrative Science Quarterly, 37*(2), 220-240.

Bazerman, M. H., Magliozzi, T., & Neale, M. A. (1985, June). Integrative bargaining in a competitive market. *Organizational Behavior and Human Decision Processes, 35*(3), 294-313.

Bazerman, M. H., Tenbrunsel, A. E., & Wade-Benzoni, K. (1998). Negotiating with yourself and losing: Making decisions with competing internal preferences. *Academy of Management Review, 23*(2), 225-241.

Bazerman, M. H., White, S. B., & Loewenstein, G. F. (1995). Perceptions of fairness in interpersonal and individual choice situations. *Current Directions in Psychological Science, 4,* 39-43.

Bazerman, M. H., Curhan, J. R., Moore, D. A., & Valley, K. L. (2000). Negotiation. *Annual Review of Psychology, 51*(1), 279-314.

Bear, J. B., & Babcock, L. (2012). Negotiation topic as a moderator or gender differences in negotiation. *Psychological Science, 23*(7), 743-744.

Beckes, L., Coan, J. A., & Hasselmo, K. (2012). Familiarity promotes the blurring of self and other in the neural representation of threat. *Social Cognitive and Affective Neuroscience, 8*(6), 670-677.

Ben-Yoav, O., & Pruitt, D. G. (1984, December). Accountability to constituents: A two-edged sword. *Organizational Behavior and Human Performance, 34*(3), 283-295.

Ben-Yoav, O., & Pruitt, D. G. (1984a, July). Resistance to yielding and the expectation of cooperative future interaction in negotiation. *Journal of Experimental Social Psychology, 20*(4), 323-335.

Bernoulli, D. (1954, January). Exposition of a new theory on the measurement of risk. *Econometrica, 22*(1), 22-36. doi:doi:10.2307/1909829

Blau, F. D., & Kahn, L. M. (2017). The gender wage gap: Extent, trends, and explanations. *Journal of Economic Literature, 55*(3), 789-865.

Boles, T. L., Croson, R. T., & Murnighan, J. K. (2000). Deception and retribution in repeated ultimatum bargaining. *Organizational Behavior and Human Decision Processes, 83*(2), 235-259.

Bottom, W. P. (1998, November). Negotiator risk: Sources of uncertainty and the impat of reference points on negotiated agreements. *Organizational Behavior and Human Decision Processes, 76*(2), 89-112.

Bottom, W. P., & Studt, A. (1993, February). Framing effects and the distributive aspect of integrative bargaining. *Organizational Behavior and Human Decision Processes, 56*, 459–474.

Bottom, W. P., Holloway, J., Miller, G. J., Mislin, A., & Whitford, A. (2006). Building a pathway for cooperation: Negotiation and social exchange between principal and agent. *Administrative Science Quarterly, 51*(1), 29–58.

Bowles, H. R., Babcock, L., & Lai, L. (2007). Social incentives for gender differences in the propensity to initiate negotiations: Sometimes it does hurt to ask. *Organizational Behavior and Human Decision Processes, 103*(1), 84–103.

Bowles, H. R., Babcock, L., & McGinn, K. L. (2005). Constraints and triggers: Situational mechanics of gender in negotiation. *Journal of Personality and Social Psychology, 89*(6), 951–965.

Bowles, H. R., Thomason, B., & Bear, J. B. (2019). Reconceptualizing what and how women negotiate for career advancement. *Academy of Management Journal, 62*(6), 1645–1671.

Brett, J. M. (2000). Culture and negotiation. *International Journal of Psychology, 35*(2), 97–104.

Brett, J. M., & Okumura, T. (1998). Inter-and intracultural negotiation: US and Japanese negotiators. *Academy of Management Journal, 41*(5), 495–510.

Brett, J., Behfar, K., & Sanchez-Burks, J. (2014). Managing cross-culture conflicts: A close look at the implication of direct versus indirect confrontation. In O. B. Ayoko, N. M. Ashkanasy, & K. A. Jehn (Eds.), *Handbook of conflict management research* (pp. 136–154). Cheltenham, UK and Northampton, MA, USA: Edward Elgar Publishing.

Brett, J. M., Gunia, B. C., & Teucher, B. M. (2017). Culture and negotiation strategy: A framework for future research. *Academy of Management Perspectives, 31*(4), 288–308.

Brett, J. M., Shapiro, D. L., & Lytle, A. L. (1996, August). Refocusing rights- and power-oriented negotiators toward integrative negotiations: Process and outcome effects. *Academy of Management Proceedings, 1*, 81–85.

Brosig, J., Ockenfels, A., & Weimann, J. (1999). How strategy sensitive are contributions. *American Economic Review, 85*(4), 891–904.

Buchan, N. R., Croson, R. T., & Dawes, R. M. (2002). Swift neighbors and persistent strangers: A cross-cultural investigation of trust and reciprocity in social exchange. *American Journal of Sociology, 108*(1), 168–206.

Byrne, D. (1962). Response to attitude similarity–dissimilarity as a function of affiliation need. *Journal of Personality, 30*(2), 164–177.

Campagna, R. L., Mislin, A. A., Kong, D. T., & Bottom, W. P. (2016). Strategic consequences of emotional misrepresentation in negotiation: The blowback effect. *Journal of Applied Psychology, 101*, 605–624.

Caputo, A., Ayoko, O. B., Amoo, N., & Menke, C. (2019). The relationship between cultural values, cultural intelligence and negotiation styles. *Journal of Business Research, 99*, 23–36.

Carnevale, P. J., & Isen, A. M. (1986, February). The influence of positive affect and visual access on the discovery of integrative solutions in bilateral negotiation. *Organizational Behavior and Human Decision Processes, 37*(1), 1–13.

Carnevale, P. J., Pruitt, D. G., & Seilheimer, S. D. (1981). Looking and competing: Accountability and visual access in integrative bargaining. *Journal of Personality and Social Psychology, 40*(1), 111–120.

Carson, T. L., Wokutch, R. E., & Murrmann, K. F. (1982). Bluffing in labor negotiation: Legal and ethical issues. *Journal of Business Ethics, 1,* 13–22.

Castillo, M., Petrie, R., Torero, M., & Vesterlund, L. (2013). Gender differences in bargaining outcomes: A field experiment on discrimination. *Journal of Public Economics, 99,* 35–48.

Chen, H. J., & Chen, Q. (2012). The mechanism of gender difference and representation role in negotiation. *Public Personnel Management, 41*(5), 91–103.

Chugh, D., Bazerman, M. H., & Banaji, M. R. (2005). Bounded ethicality as a psychological barrier to recognizing conflicts of interest. In D. A. Moore, D. M. Cain, G. Loewenstein, & M. H. Bazerman (Eds.), *Conflicts of interest: Challenges and solutions in business, law, medicine and public policy* (pp. 74–95). New York: Cambridge University Press.

Citera, M., Beauregard, R., & Mitsuya, T. (2005). An experimental study of credibility in e-negotiations. *Psychology and Marketing, 22*(2), 163–179.

Clark, H. H., & Brennan, S. E. (1991). Grounding in communication. In L. B. Resnick, J. M. Levine, & S. D. Teasley (Eds.), *Perspectives on socially shared cognition* (pp. 127–149). Worcester, MA: American Psychological Association.

Clark, M., & Mills, J. (1979). Interpersonal attraction in exchange and communal relationships. *Journal of Personality and Social Psychology, 37,* 12–24.

Cohen, T. R. (2010). Moral emotions and unethical bargaining: The differential effects of empathy and perspective taking in deterring deceitful negotiation. *Journal of Business Ethics, 94*(4), 569–579.

Cohen, T., Gunia, B., Kim-Jun, S. Y., & Murninghan, K. (2009). Do groups lie more than individuals? Honest and deception as a function of strategic self-interest. *Journal of Experimental Social Psychology, 45*(6), 1321–1324.

Cohen, T. R., Panter, A. T., Turan, N., & Kim, Y. (2014). Moral character in the workplace. *Journal of Personality and Social Psychology, 107*(5), 943–963.

Cole, S., Hideg, I., & van Kleef, G. A. (2013). The consequences of faking anger in negotiations. *Journal of Experimental Social Psychology, 49*(3), 453–463.

Coombs, C. H., & Avrunin, G. S. (1977). Single-peaked functions and the theory of preference. *Psychological Review, 84*(2), 216–230.

Cote, S., Hideg, I., & Van Kleef, G. A. (2013). The consequences of faking anger in negotiations. *Journal of Experimental Social Psychology, 49*(3), 453–463.

Croson, R. T. (1999). Look at me when you say that: An electronic negotiation simulation. *Simulation and Gaming, 30*(1), 23–37.

Cross, S. E., Bacon, P. L., & Morris, M. L. (2000). The relational-interdependent self-construal and relationships. *Journal of Personality and Social Psychology, 78*(4), 791–808.

Crossley, L., Woodworth, M., Black, P. J., & Hare, R. (2016). The dark side of negotiation: Examining the outcomes of face-to-face and computer-mediated negotiations among dark personalities. *Personality and Individual Differences, 91,* 47–51.

Crott, H., Kayser, E., & Lamm, H. (1980). The effects of information exchange and communication in an asymmetrical negotiation situation. *European Journal of Social Psychology, 10,* 149–163.

Curhan, J. R., Elfenbein, H. A., & Kilduff, G. J. (2009). Getting off on the right foot: Subjective value versus economic value in predicting longitudinal job outcomes from job offer negotiations. *Journal of Applied Psychology, 94*(2), 524-534.

Curhan, J. R., Elfenbein, H. A., & Xu, H. (2006). What do people value when they negotiate? Mapping the domain of subjective value in negotiation. *Journal of Personality and Social Psychology, 91*(3), 493-512.

Curhan, J. R., Neale, M. A., Ross, L., & Rosencranz-Engelmann, J. (2008). Relational accommodation in negotiation: Effects of egalitarianism and gender on economic efficiency and relational capital. *Organizational Behavior and Human Decision Processes, 107*(2), 192-205.

Daft, R. L., & Lengel, R. H. (1983). *Information richness: A new approach to managerial behavior and organization design*. College Station, TX: Texas A&M, College of Business Administration.

Daft, R. L., & Lengel, R. H. (1986). Organizational information requirements, media richness and structural design. *Management Science, 32*(5), 554-571.

Dannals, J. E., Zlatev, J. J., Halevy, N., & Neale, M. A. (2021). The dynamics of gender and alternatives in negotiation. *Journal of Applied Psychology*. doi: https://doi.org/10.1037/apl0000867

DeDreu, C. K., Weingart, L. R., & Kwon, S. (2000). Influence of social motives on integrative negotiation: A meta-analytic review and test of two theories. *Journal of Personality and Social Psychology, 78*(5), 889-905.

Dees, J. G., & Cramton, P. C. (1991). Shrewd bargaining on the moral frontier: Toward a theory of morality in practice. *Business Ethics Quarterly, 1*(2), 135-167.

Dees, J. G., & Cramton, P. C. (1995). Deception and mutual trust: A reply to Strudler. *Business Ethics Quarterly, 5*(4), 823-832.

Deng, Y., Wang, C. S., Aime, F., Wang, L., Sivanathan, N., & Kim, Y. C. (2021). Culture and patterns of reciprocity: The role of exchange type, regulatory focus, and emotions. Personality and *Social Psychology Bulletin, 47*(1), 20-41.

DeRue, D. S., Conlon, D. E., Moon, H., & Willaby, H. W. (2009). When is straightforwardness a liability in negotiations? The role of integrative potential and structural power. *Journal of Applied Psychology, 94*, 1032-1047.

Deutsch, M. (1973). *The resolution of conflict: Constructive and destructive processes*. New Haven, CT: Yale University Press.

Deutsch, M. (1985). *Distributive justice: A social-psychological perspective*. New Haven, CT: Yale University Press.

Dimotakis, N., Conlon, D. E., & Ilies, R. (2012). The mind and heart (literally) of the negotiator: Personality and contextual determinants of experiential reactions and economic outcomes in negotiation. *Journal of Applied Psychology, 97*(1), 183-193.

Dreber, A., & Johannesson, M. (2008). Gender differences in deception. *Economics Letters, 99*(1), 197-199.

Eagly, A. H., & Karau, S. J. (2002). Role congruity theory of prejudice toward female leaders. *Psychological Review, 109*(3), 573-598.

Earley, P. C., & Ang, S. (2003). *Cultural intelligence: Individual interactions across cultures*. Stanford, CA: Stanford University Press.

Ebner, N. (2015). Negotiation via (the new) email. In R. J. Lewicki, D. M. Saunders, & B. Barry (Eds.), *Negotiation: Readings, exercises and cases* (7th ed., pp. 188-203). New York: McGraw-Hill Education.

Elfenbein, H. A. (2015). Individual differences in negotiation: A nearly abandoned pursuit revived. *Current Directions in Psychological Science, 24*(2), 131-136.

Elfenbein, H. A. (2021). Individual differences in negotiation: A relational process model. *Organizational Psychology Review, 11*(1), 73-93.

Elfenbein, H. A., Eisenkraft, N., Curhan, J. R., & DiLalla, L. F. (2018). On the relative importance of individual-level characteristics and dyadic interaction in negotiations: Variance partitioning evidence from a twins study. *Journal of Applied Psychology, 103*(1), 88-96.

Elfenbein, H. A., Curhan, J. R., Eisenkraft, N., Shirako, A., & Baccaro, L. (2008). Are some negotiators better than others? Individual differences in bargaining outcomes. *Journal of Research in Personality, 42*(6), 1463-1475.

Epley, N., Caruso, E. M., & Bazerman, M. H. (2006). When perspective taking increases taking: Reactive egoism in social interaction. *Journal of Personality and Social Psychology, 91*(5), 872-889.

Erat, S., & Gneezy, U. (2012). White lies. *Management Science, 58*(4), 723-733.

Evans, J. (2008). Dual-processing accounts of reasoning, judgment, and social cognition. *Annual Review of Psychology, 59*, 255-278.

Exley, C. L., Niederle, M., & Vesterlund, L. (2020). Knowing when to ask: The cost of leaning in. *Journal of Political Economy, 128*(3), 816-854.

Eysenck, H. J. (1982). The biological basis of cross-cultural differences in personality: Blood group antigens. *Psychological Reports, 51*, 531-540.

Farber, H. S. (1980). An analysis of final-offer arbitration. *Journal of Conflict Resolution, 24*(4), 683-705.

Fisher, R., & Ury, W. (1981). *Getting to yes*. Boston, MA: Houghton Mifflin.

Fiske, S. T., & Taylor, S. E. (2017). *Social cognition: From brains to culture* (3rd ed.). London: Sage Publications.

Foo, M. D., Elfenbein, H. A., Tan, H. H., & Aik, V. C. (2004, April). Emotional intelligence and negotiation: The tension between creating and claiming value. *International Journal of Conflict Management, 15*(4), 411-429. doi:https://doi.org/10.1108/eb022920

Freshman, C., & Guthrie, C. (2009). Managing the goal-setting paradox: How to get better results from high goals and be happy. *Negotiation Journal, 25*(2), 217-231.

Friedman, R. A., & Currall, S. C. (2003). Conflict escalation: Dispute exacerbating elements of e-mail communication. *Human Relations, 56*(11), 1325-1347.

Friedman, R., Anderson, C., Brett, J., Olekalns, M., Goates, N., & Lisco, C. (2004). The positive and negative effects of anger on dispute resolution: Evidence from electronically mediated disputes. *Journal of Applied Psychology, 89*(2), 369-376.

Froman, L. A., & Cohen, M. E. (1970, March). Compromise and logroll: Comparing the efficiency of two bargaining processes. *Behavioral Science, 15*(2), 180-183.

Fry, W. R. (1985). The effect of dyad Machiavellianism and visual access on integrative bargaining outcomes. *Personality and Social Psychology Bulletin, 11*(1), 51-62.

Fry, W. R., Firestone, I. J., & Williams, D. L. (1983). Negotiation process and outcome of stranger dyads and dating couples: Do lovers lose? *Basic and Applied Social Psychology*, 4(1), 1-16.

Galinsky, A. D., & Mussweiler, T. (2001). First offers as anchors: The role of perspective-taking and negotiator focus. *Journal of Personality and Social Psychology*, 81(4), 657-669.

Galinsky, A. D., Gruenfeld, D. H., & Magee, J. C. (2003). From power to action. Journal of *Personality and Social Psychology*, 85(3), 453-466.

Galinsky, A. D., Ku, G., & Wang, C. S. (2005). Perspective-taking and self–other overlap: Fostering social bonds and facilitating social coordination. *Group Processes and Intergroup Relations*, 8(2), 109-124.

Galinsky, A. D., Mussweiler, T., & Medvec, V. H. (2002). Disconnecting outcomes and evaluations: The role of negotiator focus. *Journal of Personality and Social Psychology*, 83(5), 1131-1140.

Galinsky, A. D., Leonardelli, G. J., Okhuysen, G. A., & Mussweiler, T. (2005). Regulatory focus at the bargaining table: Promoting distributive and integrative success. *Personality and Social Psychology Bulletin*, 31(8), 1087-1098.

Galinsky, A. D., Maddux, W. W., Gilin, D., & White, J. B. (2008). Why it pays to get inside the head of your opponent: The differential effects of perspective-taking and empathy in strategic interactions. *Psychological Science*, 19(4), 378-384.

Galinsky, A. D., Seiden, V. L., Kim, P. H., & Medvec, V. H. (2002, February). The dissatisfaction of having your first offer accepted: The role of counterfactual thinking in negotiations. *Personality and Social Psychology Bulletin*, 28(2), 271-283.

Gaspar, J. P., & Schweitzer, M. E. (2013). The emotion deception model: A review of deception in negotiation and the role of emotion in deception. *Negotiation and Conflict Management Research*, 6(3), 160-179.

Gaspar, J. P., & Schweitzer, M. E. (2021). Confident and cunning: Negotiator self-efficacy promotes deception in negotiations. *Journal of Business Ethics*, 171(1), 139-155.

Gaspar, J. P., Levine, E. E., & Schweitzer, M. E. (2015). Why we should lie. *Organizational Dynamics*, 44(4), 306-309.

Gaspar, J. P., Methasani, R., & Schweitzer, M. (2019, February 28). Fifty shades of deception: Characteristics and consequences of lying in negotiations. *Academy of Management Perspectives*, 33(1), 62-81.

Geiger, I. (2014). Media effects on the formation of negotiator satisfaction: The example of face-to-face and text based electronically mediated negotiations. *Group Decision and Negotiation*, 23(4), 735-763.

Geiger, I. (2020). From letter to Twitter: A systematic review of communication media in negotiation. *Group Decision and Negotiation*, 29(2), 207-250.

Gelfand, M. J., & Realo, A. (1999). Individualism–collectivism and accountability in intergroup negotiations. *Journal of Applied Psychology*, 84(5), 721-736.

Gelfand, M. J., Severance, L., & Fulmer, C. A. (2012). Explaining and predicting cultural differences in negotiation. In G. Bolton, & R. Croson (Eds.), *Handbook of negotiation: Experimental economic perspectives* (pp. 332-356). New York: Oxford University Press.

Gelfand, M. J., Gordon, S., Li, C., Choi, V., & Prokopowicz, P. (2018). One reason mergers fail: The two cultures aren't compatible. *Harvard Business Review*, 1-4.

Gelfand, M. J., Smith Major, V., Raver, J. L., Nishii, L. H., & O'Brien, K. (2006, April). Negotiating relationally: The dynamics of the relational self in negotiations. *Academy of Management Review, 31*(2), 427-451.

Gelfand, M. J., Raver, J. L., Nishii, L., Leslie, L. M., Lun, J., Lim, B. C., ... Yamaguchi, S. (2011, May 27). Differences between tight and loose cultures: A 33-nation study. *Science, 332*(6033), 1100-1104.

George, J. M., Jones, G. R., & Gonzalez, J. A. (1998). The role of affect in cross-cultural negotiations. *Journal of International Business Studies, 29*(4), 749-772.

Giacomantonio, M., Ten Velden, F. S., & DeDreu, C. K. (2016). Framing effortful strategies as easy enables depleted individuals to execute complex tasks effectively. *Journal of Experimental Social Psychology, 62*, 68-74.

Gilin, D., Maddux, W. W., Carpenter, J., & Galinsky, A. D. (2013). When to use your head and when to use your heart: The differential value of perspective-taking versus empathy in competitive interactions. *Personality and Social Psychology Bulletin, 39*(1), 3-16.

Gino, F., Ayal, S., & Ariely, D. (2009). Contagion and differentiation in unethical behavior. *Psychological Science, 20*(3), 393-398.

Giordano, G. A., Stoner, J. S., Brouer, R. L., & George, J. F. (2007). The influences of deception and computer-mediation on dyadic negotiations. *Journal of Computer-Mediated Communication, 12*(2), 362-383.

Glick, S., & Croson, R. (2001). Reputations in negotiation. In S. Hoch, & H. Kunreuther (Eds.), *Wharton on decision making* (pp. 177-186). New York: Wiley.

Gneezy, U. (2005). Deception: The role of consequences. *American Economic Review, 95*(1), 384-394.

Graham, J. L. (1985). The influence of culture on the process of business negotiations: An exploratory study. *Journal of International Business Studies, 16*(1), 81-96.

Greenhalgh, L., & Neslin, S. (1983). Determining outcomes of negotiation: An empirical assessment. In M. H. Bazerman, & R. J. Lewicki (Eds.), *Negotiating in organizations* (pp. 114-134). Thousand Oaks, CA: Sage Publications.

Groves, K. S., Feverherm, A., & Gu, M. (2015). Examining cultural intelligence and cross-cultural negotiation effectiveness. *Journal of Management Education, 39*(2), 209-243.

Gunia, B. C. (2019). Ethics in negotiation: Causes and consequences. *Academy of Management Perspective, 33*(1), 3-11.

Gunia, B. C., Brett, J. M., & Gelfand, M. J. (2016). The science of culture and negotiation. *Current Opinion in Psychology, 8*, 78-83.

Gunia, B. C., Brett, J. M., Nandkeolyar, A. K., & Kamdar, D. (2011). Paying a price: Culture, trust and negotiation consequences. *Journal of Applied Psychology, 96*(4), 774-789.

Hall, E. T. (1976). *Beyond culture*. Garden City, NY: Anchor Books.

Hamner, W. C. (1980). The influence of structural, individual, and strategic differences. In D. L. Harnett, & L. L. Cummings (Eds.), *Bargaining behavior: An international study* (pp. 21-80). Houston, TX: Dame.

Harris, K. L., & Carnevale, P. (1990, October). Chilling and hastening: The influence of third-party power and interests on negotiation. *Organizational Behavior and Human Decision Processes*, 47(1), 138-160.

Harsanyi, J. C. (1962). Bargaining in ignorance of the opponent's utility function. *Journal of Conflict Resolution*, 6, 29-38.

Harsanyi, J. C. (1990). Bargaining. In J. Eatwell, M. Milgate, & P. Newman (Eds.), *The new Palgrave: A dictionary of economics* (pp. 54-67). New York: Norton.

Haselhuhn, M. P., & Wong, E. M. (2012). Bad to the bone: Facial structure predicts unethical behaviour. *Proceedings of the Royal Society B: Biological Sciences*, 279(1728), 571-576.

Henrich, J., Heine, S. J., & Norenzayan, A. (2010). The weirdest people in the world? *Behavioral and Brain Sciences*, 33(2-3), 61-83.

Herodotus (2003). *The histories*, trans. by A. Selincourt. London: Penguin Classics.

Hideg, I., & van Kleef, G. A. (2017). When expressions of fake emotions elicit negative reactions: The role of observers' dialectical thinking. *Journal of Organizational Behavior*, 38(8), 1196-1212.

Higgins, E. T. (1998). Promotion and prevention: Regulatory focus as a motivational principle. In M. P. Zanna (Ed.), *Advances in experimental social psychology* (pp. 1-46). New York: Academic Press.

Higgins, E. T. (2005). Value from regulatory fit. *Current Directions in Psychological Science*, 14(4), 209-213.

Hilty, J. A., & Carnevale, P. J. (1993). Black-hat/white-hat strategy in bilateral negotiation. *Organizational Behavior and Human Decision Processes*, 55(3), 444-469.

Hoffman, D. A. (2011). Mediation and the art of shuttle diplomacy. *Negotiation Journal*, 27(3), 263-309.

Hofstede, G. (1986). Cultural differences in teaching and learning. *International Journal of Intercultural Relations*, 10(3), 301-320.

Holt, J. L., & DeVore, C. J. (2005). Culture, gender, organizational role, and styles on conflict resolution: A meta-analysis. *International Journal of Intercultural Relations*, 29(2), 165-196.

Hong, A. P., & van der Wijst, P. J. (2013). Women in negotiation: Effects of gender and power on negotiation behavior. *Negotiation and Conflict Management Research*, 6(4), 273-284.

House, R. J., Hanges, P. J., Javidan, M., Dorfman, P. W., & Gupta, V. (Eds.) (2004). *Culture, leadership, and organizations: The GLOBE study of 62 societies*. London: Sage Publications.

Huber, V. L., & Neale, M. A. (1986). Effects of cognitive heuristics and goals on negotiator performance and subsequent goal setting. *Organizational Behavior and Human Decision Processes*, 38(2), 342-365.

Hui, C. H., & Triandis, H. C. (1986). Individualism–collectivism: A study of cross-cultural researchers. *Journal of Cross-Cultural Psychology*, 17(2), 225-248.

Imai, L., & Gelfand, M. J. (2010). The culturally intelligent negotiator: The impact of cultural intelligence (CQ) on negotiation sequences and outcomes. *Organizational Behavior and Human Decision Processes*, 112(2), 83-98.

Isen, A. M. (1999). On the relationship between affect and creative problem solving. In S. W. Ross (Ed.), *Affect, creative experience and psychological adjustment* (Vol. 3, pp. 3-17). London: Taylor & Francis.

Isen, A. M. (2000). Positive affect and decision making. In M. Lewis, & J. M. Haviland-Jones (Eds.), *Handbook of emotions* (2nd ed., pp. 417-435). New York: Guilford Press.

Isen, A. M. (2001). An influence of positive affect on decision making in complex sitations: Theoretical issues with practical implications. *Journal of Consumer Psychology, 11*(2), 75-85.

Isen, A. M. (2002a). Missing in action in the AIM: Positive affect's facilitation of cognitive flexibility, innovation, and problem solving. *Psychological Inquiry, 13*(1), 57-65.

Isen, A. M. (2002b). A role for neuropsychology in understanding the facilitating influence of positive affect of social behavior and cognitive processes. In C. R. Snyder, & S. J. Lopez (Eds.), *Handbook of positive psychology* (pp. 528-540). New York: Oxford University Press.

Isen, A. M. (2004). Some perspectives on positive feelings and emotions: Positive affect facilitates thinking and problem solving. In A. R. Manstead, N. Frijda, & A. Fischer (Eds.), *Feelings and emotions: The Amsterdam symposium* (pp. 263-281). New York: Cambridge University Press.

Isen, A. M., & Labroo, A. A. (2003). Some ways in which positive affect facilitates decision making and judgment. In S. Schneider, & J. Shanteau (Eds.), Cambridge series on judgment and decision making. *Emerging perspectives on judgment and decision research* (pp. 365-393). Cambridge, MA: Cambridge University Press.

Isen, A. M., Daubman, K. A., & Nowicki, G. P. (1987). Positive affect facilitates creative problem solving. *Journal of Personality and Social Psychology, 52*(6), 1121-1131.

Jazaieri, H., & Kray, L. J. (2020). Deception in negotiations: The unique role of gender. In M. Olekalns, & J. A. Kennedy (Eds.), *Handbook on gender and negotiation* (pp. 93-109). Cheltenham, UK and Northampton, MA, USA: Edward Elgar Publishing.

John, O. P., Donahue, E. M., & Kentle, R. L. (1991). *Big five inventory*. APA PsycTests. https://doi.org/10.1037/t07550-000

Johnson, N. A., & Cooper, R. B. (2009). Media, affect, concession, and agreement in negotiation: IM versus telephone. *Decision Support Systems, 46*(3), 673-684.

Kahneman, D. (2011). *Thinking, fast and slow* (1st ed.). New York: Farrar, Straus and Giroux.

Kahneman, D., & Tversky, A. (1973, July). On the psychology of prediction. *Psychological Review, 80*(4), 237-251.

Kahneman, D., & Tversky, A. (1979). Prospect theory: An analysis of decision under risk. *Econometrica, 47*(2), 263-291.

Kahneman, D., Slovic, P., & Tversky, A. (Eds.) (1982). *Judgment under uncertainty: Heuristics and biases*. Cambridge, UK: Cambridge University Press.

Kapoutsis, I., Volkema, R. J., & Nikolopoulos, A. G. (2013). Initiating negotiations: The role of Machiavellianism, risk propensity, and bargaining power. *Group Decision and Negotiation, 22*(6), 1081-1101.

Kelley, H. H. (1966). A classroom study of the dilemmas in interpersonal negotiations. In K. Archibald (Ed.), *Strategic interaction and conflict* (pp. 49-73).
Berkeley, CA: University of California Institute of International Studies.

Kelley, H. H., & Schenitzki, D. P. (1972). Bargaining. In C. McClintock (Ed.),
Experimental social psychology (pp. 298-337). New York: Holt, Rinehart, &
Winston.

Kelley, H. H., & Stahelski, A. J. (1970). Social interaction basis of cooperators' and
competitors' beliefs about others. *Journal of Personality and Social Psychology,*
16(1), 66-91.

Kelley, H. H., & Thibaut, J. W. (1969). Group problem solving. In G. Lindzey, &
E. Aronson (Eds.), *The handbook of social psychology* (2nd ed.). Reading, MA:
Addison-Wesley.

Keltner, D., Gruenfeld, D. H., & Anderson, C. (2003). Power, approach, and inhi-
bition. *Psychological Review, 110*(2), 265-284.

Kemp, K. E., & Smith, W. P. (1994). Information exchange, toughness, and
integrative bargaining: The roles of explicit cues and perspective-taking.
International Journal of Conflict Management, 5(1), 5-21. doi:https://doi.org/
10.1108/eb022734

Kennedy, J. A., Kray, L. J., & Ku, G. (2017). A social-cognitive approach to understanding gender differences in negotiator ethics: The role of moral identity.
Organizational Behavior and Human Decision Processes, 138, 28-44.

Kenny, D. A., & La Voie, L. (1984). The social relations model. In L. Berkowitz
(Ed.), *Advances in experimental social psychology* (Vol. 18, pp. 141-182). New
York: Academic Press.

Kern, M. C., & Chugh, D. (2009). Bounded ethicality: The perils of loss framing.
Psychological Science, 20(3), 378-384.

Kim, H., & Markus, H. R. (1999). Deviance or uniqueness, harmony, or conform-
ity? A cultural analysis. *Journal of Personality and Social Psychology, 77*(4),
785-800.

Kim, K., Cundiff, N. L., & Choi, S. B. (2014). The influence of emotional intelligence on negotiation outcomes and the mediating effect of rapport: A structural equation modeling approach. *Negotiation Journal, 30*(1), 49-68.

Kish-Gephart, J. J., Harrison, D. A., & Trevino, L. K. (2010). Bad apples, bad cases,
and bad barrels: Meta-analytic evidence about sources of unethical decisions at
work. *Journal of Applied Psychology, 95*(1), 1-31.

Kong, D. T., Dirks, K. T., & Ferrin, D. L. (2014). Interpersonal trust within negotiations: Meta-analytic evidence, critical contingencies, and directions for future
research. *Academy of Management Journal, 57*(5), 1235-1255.

Koning, L., Van Dijk, E., Van Beest, I., & Steinel, W. (2010). An instrumental
account of deception on reactions to deceit in bargaining. *Business Ethics*
Quarterly, 20, 57-73.

Kopelman, S., & Rosette, A. S. (2008). Cultural variation in response to strategic
emotions in negotiations. *Group Decision and Negotiation, 17*(1), 65-77.

Kopelman, S., Rosette, A. S., & Thompson, L. L. (2006). The three faces of Eve.
Organizational Behavior and Human Decision Processes, 99(1), 81-101.

Kouchaki, M., & Kray, L. J. (2018). "I won't let you down:" Personal ethical lapses
arising from women's advocating for others. *Organizational Behavior and*
Human Decision Processes, 147, 147-157.

Krasikova, D. V., & LeBreton, J. M. (2012). Just the two of us: Misalignment of theory and methods in examining dyadic phenomena. *Journal of Applied Psychology*, *97*(4), 739-757.

Krauss, R. M., & Chiu, C. Y. (1998). Language and social behavior. In D. T. Gilbert, S. T. Fiske, & G. Lindzey (Eds.), *The handbook of social psychology* (pp. 41-88). New York: McGraw-Hill.

Kray, L. J., & Gelfand, M. J. (2009). Relief versus regret: The effect of gender and negotiating norm ambiguity on reactions to having one's first offer accepted. *Social Cognition*, *27*(3), 418-436.

Kray, L. J., & Haselhuhn, M. P. (2007). Implicit negotiation beliefs and performance: Experimental and longitudinal evidence. *Journal of Personality and Social Psychology*, *93*(1), 49-64.

Kray, L. J., & Haselhuhn, M. P. (2008). What it takes to succeed: An examination of the relationship between negotiators' implicit beliefs and performance. *Leadership at the Crossroads: Leadership and Psychology*, *1*, 213-229.

Kray, L. J., & Haselhuhn, M. P. (2012). Male pragmatism in negotiators' ethical reasoning. *Journal of Experimental Social Psychology*, *48*(5), 1124-1131.

Kray, L. J., Galinsky, A. D., & Thompson, L. (2002). Reversing the gender gap in negotiations: An exploration of stereotype regeneration. *Organizational Behavior and Human Decision Processes*, *87*(2), 386-409.

Kray, L. J., Kennedy, J. A., & Van Zant, A. B. (2014, November). Not competent enough to know the difference? Gender stereotypes about women's ease of being misled predict negotiator deception. *Organizational Behavior and Human Decision Processes*, *125*(2), 61-72.

Kray, L. J., Paddock, L., & Galinsky, A. D. (2008). The effect of past performance on expected control and risk attitudes in integrative negotiations. *Negotiation and Conflict Management Research*, *1*(2), 161-178.

Kray, L. J., Thompson, L., & Galinsky, A. (2001). Battle of the sexes: Gender stereotype confirmation and reactance in negotiations. *Journal of Personality and Social Psychology*, *80*(6), 942-958.

Kray, L. J., Thompson, L. L., & Lind, E. A. (2005, September). It's a bet! A problem-solving approach promotes the construction of contingent agreements. *Personality and social Psychology Bulletin*, *31*(8), 1039-1051.

Kray, L. J., Reb, J., Galinsky, A. D., & Thompson, L. L. (2004). Stereotype reactance at the bargaining table: the effect of stereotype activation and power on claiming and creating value. *Personality and social Psychology Bulletin*, *30*(4), 399-411.

Kreve, M. E. (2016). *Uncertainty and behaviour: Perceptions, decisions and actions in business*. London: Routledge.

Kristof-Brown, A. L., Zimmerman, R. D., & Johnson, E. C. (2005). Consequences of individual's fit at work: A meta-analysis of person–job, person–organization, person–group, and person–supervisor fit. *Personnel Psychology*, *58*(2), 281-342.

Ku, G., Wang, C. S., & Galinsky, A. D. (2015). The promise and perversity of perspective-taking in organizations. *Research in Organizational Behavior*, *35*, 79-102.

Kugler, K. G., Reif, J. A., Kaschner, T., & Brodbeck, F. C. (2018). Gender differences in the initiation of negotiations: A meta-analysis. *Psychological Bulletin*, *144*(2), 198-222.

Kurtzberg, T., & Medvec, V. H. (1999). Can we negotiate and still be friends? *Negotiation Journal*, *15*, 355–361.

Kwon, S., & Weingart, L. R. (2004). Unilateral concession from the other party: Concession behavior, attributions, and negotiation judgments. *Journal of Applied Psychology*, *89*(2), 263–278.

Laubert, C., & Parlamis, J. (2019). Are you angry (happy, sad) or aren't you? Emotion detection difficulty in email negotiation. *Group Decision and Negotiation*, *28*(2), 377–413.

Lax, D. A., & Sebenius, J. K. (1986). *The manager as negotiator*. New York: The Free Press.

Lazarus, R. S. (1991). *Emotion and adaptation*. New York: Oxford University Press.

Lee, A. J., & Ames, D. R. (2017). "I can't pay more" versus "It's not worth more": Divergent effects of constraint and disparagement rationales in negotiations. *Organizational Behavior and Human Decision Processes*, *141*, 16–28.

Lee, M., Pitesa, M., Pillutla, M. M., & Thau, S. (2017). Male immorality: An evolutionary account of sex differences in unethical negotiation behavior. *Academy of Management Journal*, *60*(5), 2014–2044.

Lee, S., Adair, W. L., & Seo, S. J. (2013). Cultural perspective taking in cross-cultural negotiation. *Group Decision and Negotiation*, *22*(3), 389–405.

Leibbrandt, A., & List, J. A. (2015). Do women avoid salary negotiations? Evidence from a large-scale natural field experiment. *Management Science*, *61*(9), 2016–2024.

Levine, E. E., & Schweitzer, M. E. (2014). Are liars ethical? On the tension between benevolence and honesty. *Journal of Experimental Social Psychology*, *53*, 107–117.

Levine, E. E., & Schweitzer, M. E. (2015, January). Prosocial lies: When deception breeds trust. *Organizational Behavior and Human Decision Processes*, *126*, 88–106.

Levy, J. S. (1997, March). Prospect theory, rational choice, and international relations. *International Studies Quarterly*, *41*(1), 87–112.

Lewicki, R. J. (1983). Lying and deception: A behavior model. In Bazerman M. H. & R. J. Lewicki (Eds.), *Negotiating in organizations* (pp. 68–90). Newbury Park: Sage Publications.

Lewicki, R. J., & Bunker, B. B. (1996). Developing and maintaining trust in work relationships. In R. M. Kramer, & R. R. Tyler (Eds.), *Trust in organizations: Frontiers of theory and research* (pp. 1114–1139). Thousand Oaks, CA: Sage Publications.

Lewicki, R., & Polin, B. (2013, September). The role of trust in negotiation processes. In R. Bachmann, & A. Zaheer (Eds.), *Handbook of advances in trust research* (pp. 29–54). Cheltenham, UK and Northampton, MA, USA: Edward Elgar Publishing.

Lewicki, R. J., & Stark, N. (1996, March). What is ethically appropriate in negotiations: An empirical examination of bargaining tactics. *Social Justice Research*, *9*(1), 69–95.

Lewicki, R. J., Litterer, J. A., Saunders, D., & Minton, J. (1985). *Negotiation*. Homewood, IL: Richard D. Irwin Publishers.

Lewis, S. A., & Fry, W. R. (1977). Effects of visual access and orientation on the discovery of integrative bargaining alternatives. *Organizational Behavior and Human Performance, 20*(1), 75-92.

Liberman, V., Samuels, S. M., & Ross, L. (2004). The name of the game: Predictive power of reputations versus situational labels in determining prisoner's dilemma game moves. *Personality and Social Psychology Bulletin, 30,* 1175-1185.

Lind, E. A., & Tyler, T. R. (1988). *The social psychology of procedural justice.* New York: Plenum Press.

Liu, L. A., Friedman, R., Barry, B., Gelfand, M. J., & Zhang, Z. X. (2012, June). The dynamics of consensus building in intracultural and intercultural negotiations. *Administrative Science Quarterly, 57*(2), 269-304.

Liu, W., Friedman, R., & Hong, Y. Y. (2012). Culture and accountability in negotiation: Recognizing the importance of in-group relations. *Organizational Behavior and Human Decision Processes, 117*(1), 221-234.

Locke, E. A., & Latham, G. P. (1990). *A theory of goal setting & task performance.* Englewood Cliffs, NJ: Prentice Hall.

Loewenstein, G. F., Thompson, L., & Bazerman, M. H. (1989). Social utility and decision making in interpersonal contexts. *Journal of Personality and Social Psychology, 57*(3), 426-441. http://dx.doi.org/10.1037/0022-3514.57.3.426

Long, E. C. (1994). Maintaining a stable marriage: Perspective taking as a predictor or a propensity to divorce. *Journal of Divorce and Remarriage, 21*(1-2), 121-138.

Loschelder, D., Friese, M., & Trotschel, R. (2017). How and why precise anchors distinctly affect anchor recipients and senders. *Journal of Experimental Social Psychology, 70,* 164-176.

Loschelder, D. D., Trotschel, R., Swaab, R. I., Friese, M., & Galinsky, A. D. (2016). The information-anchoring model of first offers: When moving first helps versus hurts negotiators. *Journal of Applied Psychology, 101*(7), 995-1012.

Lugger, K., Geiger, I., Neun, H., & Backhaus, K. (2015). When East meets West at the bargaining table: Adaptation, behavior and outcomes in intra-and intercultural German–Chinese business negotiations. *Journal of Business Economics, 85*(1), 15-43.

Lundquist, T., Ellingsen, T., Gribbe, E., & Johannesson, M. (2009). The aversion to lying. *Journal of Economic Behavior and Organization, 70*(1-2), 81-92.

Maaravi, Y., & Levy, A. (2017, September). When your anchor sinks your boat: Information asymmetry in distributive negotiations and the disadvantage of making the first offer. *Judgment and Decision Making, 12*(5), 420-429.

Maaravi, Y., Pazy, A., & Ganzach, Y. (2014). Winning a battle but losing the war: On the drawbacks of using the anchoring tactic in distributive negotiations. *Judgment and Decision Making, 9*(6), 548-557.

Malhotra, D., & Gino, F. (2011). The pursuit of power corrupts: How investing in outside options motivates opportunism in relationships. *Administrative Science Quarterly, 56*(4), 559-592.

Mandel, D. R. (2006). Economic transactions among friends. *Journal of Conflict Resolution, 50*(4), 584-606.

Markus, H. R., & Kitavama, S. (2010). Cultures and selves: A cycle of mutual constitution. *Perspectives on Psychological Science, 5*(4), 420-430.

Mason, M. F., Lee, A. J., Wiley, E. A., & Ames, D. R. (2013). Precise offers are potent anchors: Conciliatory counteroffers and attributions of knowledge in negotiations. *Journal of Experimental Social Psychology, 49*(4), 759-763.

Matsumoto, D., Yoo, S. H., & Nakagawa, S. (2008). Culture, emotion regulation, and adjustment. *Journal of Personality and Social Psychology, 94*(6), 925-937.

Mayer, D. M., Aquino, K., Greenbaum, R. L., & Kuenzi, M. (2012). Who displays ethical leadership, and why does it matter? An examination of antecedents and consequences of ethical leadership. *Academy of Management Journal, 55*(1), 151-171.

Mazei, J., Huffmeier, J., Freund, P. A., Stuhlmacher, A. F., Bilke, L., & Hertel, G. (2015). A meta-analysis on gender differences in negotiation outcomes and their moderators. *Psychological Bulletin, 141*(1), 85-104.

McClelland, G., & Rohrbaugh, J. (1978). Who accepts the pareto axiom? The role of utility and equity in arbitration decisions. *Behavioral Science, 23*(5), 446-456.

McClintock, C. G., & van Avermaet, E. (1982). Social values and rules of fairness: A theoretical perspective. In V. J. Derlega, & J. Grzelak (Eds.), *Cooperation and helping behavior* (pp. 43-71). New York: Academic Press.

McGinn, K. L. (2006). Relationships and negotations in context. In L. Thompson (Ed.), *Negotiation theory and research: Frontiers of social psychology* (pp. 129-144). New York: Psychology Press.

McGinn, K. L., & Keros, A. T. (2002). Improvisation and the logic of exchange in socially embedded transactions. *Administrative Science Quarterly, 47*, 442-473.

McGinn, K. L., Thompson, L., & Bazerman, M. H. (2003). Dyadic processes of disclosure and reciprocity in bargaining with communication. *Journal of Behavioral Decision Making, 16*(1), 17-34.

McGraw, A. P., & Tetlock, P. E. (2005). Taboo trade-offs, relational framing, and the acceptability of exchanges. *Journal of Consumer Psychology, 15*(1), 2-15.

McPherson, M., Smith-Lovin, L., & Cook, J. M. (2001). Birds of a feather: Homophily in social networks. *Annual Review of Sociology, 27*(1), 415-444.

Messick, D. M., & Bazerman, M. H. (1996). Ethics for the 21st century: A decision making approach. *Sloam Management Review, 37*, 9-22.

Messick, D. M., & McClintock, C. G. (1968). Motivational bases of choice in experimental games. *Journal of Experimental Social Psychology, 4*(1), 1-25.

Messick, D. M., & Sentis, K. P. (1979, July). Fairness and preference. *Journal and Experimental Social Psychology, 15*(4), 418-434. Retrieved from https://doi.org/10.1016/0022-1031(79)90047-7

Minson, J. A., Ruedy, N. E., & Schweitzer, M. E. (2011). Ask (the right way) and you shall receive: The effect of question type on information disclosure and deception. *Academy of Management Meeting.* San Antonio, TX.

Moran, S., & Schweitzer, M. E. (2008). When better is worse: Envy and the use of deception. *Negotiation and Conflict Management Research, 1*, 3-29.

Morley, I. E., & Stephenson, G. M. (1969). Interpersonal and inter-party exchange: A laboratory simulation of an industrial negotiation at the plant level. *British Journal of Psychology, 60*(4), 543-545.

Morley, I., &. Stephenson, G. M. (1977). *The social psychology of bargaining.* New York: Psychology Press.

Morris, M. W., Hong, Y. Y., Chiu, C. Y., & Liu, Z. (2015). Normology: Integrating insights about social norms to understand cultural dynamics. *Organizational Behavior and Human Decision Processes, 129*, 1-13.

Morse, L., & Cohen, T. R. (2019). Moral character in negotiation. *Academy of Management Perspectives, 33*(1), 12-25.

Murnighan, J. K., Cantelon, D. A., & Elyashiv, T. (2001). Bounded personal ethics and the tap dance of real estate agency. In J. A. Wagner, J. M. Bartunek, & K. D. Elsback (Eds.), *Advances in qualitative organizational research* (Vol. 3, pp. 1-40). New York: Elsevier/JAI.

Murnighan, J. K., Babcock, L., Thompson, L., & Pillutla, M. M. (1999). The information dilemma in negotiations: Effects of experience, incentives, and integrative potential. *International Journal of Conflict Management, 10*, 313-339.

Myerson, R. B. (1991a). Analysis of incentives in bargaining and mediation. In H. P. Young (Ed.), *Negotiation analysis* (pp. 67-85). Ann Arbor, MI: The University of Michigan Press.

Myerson, R. B. (1991b). *Game theory: Analysis of conflict.* Cambridge, MA: Harvard University Press.

Nash, J. (1950). The bargaining problem. *Econometrica, 18*, 155-162.

Nash, J. (1951, September). Non-cooperative games. *Annals of Mathematics, 54*(2), 286-295.

Neale, M. A., & Bazerman, M. H. (1983). The role of perspective-taking ability in negotiating under different forms of arbitration. *ILR Review, 36*(3), 378-388.

Neale, M. A., & Bazerman, M. H. (1985, January). The effect of externally set goals on reaching integrative agreements in competitive markets. *Journal of Organizational Behavior, 6*(1), 19-32.

Neale, M. A., & Bazerman, M. H. (1991). *Cognition and rationality in negotiation.* New York: Free Press.

Neale, M. A., & Northcraft, G. (1986). Experts, amateurs, and refrigerators: Comparing expert and amateur negotiators in a novel task. *Organizational Behavior and Human Decision Processes, 38*, 305-317.

Neale, M. A., Huber, V. L., & Northcraft, G. B. (1987). The framing of negotiations: Contextual versus task frames. *Organizational Behavior and Human Decision Processes, 39*(2), 228-241.

O'Connor, K. M., & Carnevale, P. J. (1997). A nasty but effective negotiation strategy: Misrepresentation of a common-value issue. *Personality and Social Psychology Bulletin, 23*(5), 504-515.

O'Connor, K. M., Arnold, J. A., & Burris, E. R. (2005). Negotiators' bargaining histories and their effects on future negotiation performance. *Journal of Applied Psychology, 90*(2), 350-362.

O'Connor, K. M., Arnold, J. A., & Maurizio, A. M. (2010). The prospect of negotiating: Stress, cognitive appraisal and performance. *Journal of Experimental Social Psychology, 46*(5), 729-735.

Oishi, S., & Graham, J. (2010). Social ecology: Lost and found in psychological science. *Perspectives on Psychological Science, 5*(4), 356-377.

Oishi, S., Schug, J., Yuki, M., & Axt, J. (2015). The psychology of residential and relational mobilities. In M. J. Gelfand, C.-Y. Chiu, & Y.-Y. Hong (Eds.), *Handbook of advances in culture and psychology* (Vol. 5, pp. 221-272). Oxford: Oxford University Press.

Olekalns, M., & Druckman, D. (2014). With feeling: How emotions shape negotiation. *Negotiation Journal*, *30*(4), 455–478.

O'Quinn, K., & Aronoff, J. (1981, December). Humor as a technique of social influence. *Social Psychology Quarterly*, *44*(4), 349–357.

Osgood, C. E. (1962). *An alternative to war or surrender*. Urbana, IL: University of Illinois Press.

Oskamp, S. (1965, February). Attitudes toward U.S. and Russian actions: A double standard. *Psychological Reports*, *16*(1), 43–46.

Oskamp, S., & Hartry, A. (1968). A factor-analytic study of the double standard in attitudes toward US and Russian actions. *Behavioral Science*, *13*(3), 178–188.

Pareto, V. (1906). *Manuel D' Economie Polique* (2nd ed. 1927 trans. by A. A. Schwier as Manual of Political Economy). New York: Augustus M. Kelley, 1971.

Parkinson, B. (1996, November). Emotions are social. *British Journal of Psychology*, *87*(4), 663–683.

Pearson, V. M., & Stephan, W. G. (1998). Preferences for styles of negotiation: A comparison of Brazil and the U.S. *International Journal of Intercultural Relations*, *22*(1), 67–83.

Pesendorfer, E. M., & Koeszegi, S. T. (2006). Hot versus cool behavioural styles in electronic negotiations: The impact of communication mode. *Group Decision and Negotiation*, *15*(2), 141–155.

Pierce, J. R., & Thompson, L. (2018). Explaining differences in men and women's use of unethical tactics in negotiation. *Negotiation and Conflict Management Research*, *11*(4), 278–297.

Pierce, J. R., Kilduff, G. J., Galinsky, A. D., & Sivanathan, N. (2013). From Glue to Gasoline: How competition turns perspective takers unethical. *Psychological Science*, *24*(10), 1986–1994.

Pruitt, D. G. (1981). *Negotiation behavior*. New York: Academic Press.

Pruitt, D. G., & Carnevale, P. J. (1993). *Negotiation in social conflict*. Milton Keynes: Open University Press.

Pruitt, D. G., & Lewis, S. A. (1975). Development of integrative solutions in bilateral negotiation. *Journal of Personality and Social Psychology*, *31*(4), 621–633.

Pruitt, D. G., & Rubin, J. (1986). *Social conflict: Escalation, stalemate, and settlement*. The University of Michigan, Ann Arbor: Random House.

Purdy, J. M., Nye, P., & Balakrishnan, P. S. (2000). The impact of communication media on negotiation outcomes. *International Journal of Conflict Management*, *11*(2), 162–187.

Raiffa, H. (1982). *The art and science of negotiation*. Cambridge, MA: Harvard University Press.

Ramirez-Fernandez, J., Ramirez-Marin, J. Y., & Munduate, L. (2018). I expected more from you: The influence of close relationships and perspective taking on negotiation offers. *Group Decision and Negotiation*, *27*(1), 85–105.

Rees, M. R., Tenbrunsel, A. E., & Bazerman, M. H. (2019). Bounded ethicality and ethical fading in negotiations: Understanding unintended unethical behavior. *Academy of Management Perspectives*, *33*(1), 26–42.

Reinders Folmer, C. P., & De Cremer, D. (2012, February). Bad for me or bad for us? Interpersonal orientations and the impact of losses on unethical behavior. *Personality and social Psychology Bulletin*, *38*(6), 760–771.

Robertson, D. C., & Rymon, T. (2001). Purchasing agents' deceptive behavior: A randomized response technique study. *Business Ethics Quarterly, 11*(3), 455-479.

Robinson, R. J., & Keltner, D. (1996). Much ado about nothing? Revisionists and traditionalists choose an introductory English syllabus. *Psychological Science, 7*(1), 18-24.

Robinson, R. J., Lewicki, R. J., & Donahue, E. M. (2000). Extending and testing a five factor model of ethical and unethical bargaining tactics: Introducing the SINS scale. *Journal of Organizational Behavior, 21*(6), 649-664.

Rogers, T., Zeckhauser, R., Gino, F., Norton, M. I., & Schweitzer, M. E. (2017). Artful paltering: The risks and rewards of using truthful statements to mislead others. *Journal of Personality and Social Psychology, 112*, 456-473.

Rosette, A. S., Brett, J. M., Barsness, Z., & Lytle, A. L. (2012). When cultures clash electronically: The impact of email and social norms on negotiation behavior and outcomes. *Journal of Cross-Cultural Psychology, 43*(4), 628-643.

Ross, L., & Stillinger, C. (1988). *Psychological barriers to conflict resolution* (Vol. 4). Berkeley, CA: Stanford Center on Conflict and Negotiation, Stanford University.

Ross, L., & Stillinger, C. (1991, October). Barriers to conflict resolution. *Negotiation Journal, 7*(4)389-404.

Roth, A. E. (1995). Bargaining experiments. In J. H. Kagel, & A. E. Roth (Eds.), *The handbook of experimental economics* (pp. 253-348). Princeton, NJ: Princeton University Press.

Rousseau, D., Sitkin, S., Burt, R., & Camerer, C. (1998, July). Not so different after all: A cross-discipline view of trust. *Academy of Management Review, 23*(3), 393-404.

Rubin, J. Z., & Brown, B. R. (1975). *The social psychology of bargaining and negotiation.* New York: Academic Press.

Rubin, J. Z., & Brown, B. R. (2013). *The social psychology of bargaining and negotiation.* Amsterdam: Elsevier.

Rubin, J. Z., & Sander, F. A. (1988). When should we use agents: Direct vs. representative negotiation. *Negotiation Journal, 4*, 395-401.

Rudman, L. A., & Mescher, K. (2013). Penalizing men who request a family leave: Is flexibility stigma a femininity stigma. *Journal of Social Issues, 69*(2), 322-340.

Sauer, C., Valet, P., Shams, S., & Tomaskovic-Devey, D. (2021, September 13). Categorical distinctions and claims making: Opportunity, agency, and returns from wage negotiations. *American Sociological Review, 86*(5), 934-959. doi: https://doi.org/10.1177/00031224211038507

Savage, L. J. (1954). *The foundations of statistics.* New York: John Wiley and Sons.

Schelling, T. (1960). *The strategy of conflict.* Cambridge, MA: Harvard University Press.

Schoeninger, D. W., & Wood, W. D. (1969). Comparison of marreid and ad hoc mixed-sex dyads negotiating the division of a reward. *Journal of Experimental Social Psychology, 5*(4), 483-499.

Schwartz, S. (2006). A theory of cultural value orientations: Explication and applications. *Comparative Sociology, 5*(2-3), 137-182.

Schweinsberg, M., Ku, G., Wang, C. S., & Pillutla, M. M. (2012, January). Starting high and ending with nothing: The role of anchors and power in negotiations. *Journal of Experimental Social Psychology, 48*(1), 226-231.

Schweitzer, M. E., & Croson, R. (1999, March). Curtailing deception: The impact of direct questions on lies and omissions. *International Journal of Conflict Management, 10*(3), 225-248.

Schweitzer, M. E., & Hsee, C. K. (2002). Stretching the truth: Elastic justification and motivated communication of uncertain information. *Journal of Risk and Uncertainty, 25*(2), 185-201.

Schweitzer, M. E., DeChurch, L., & Gibson, D. (2005). Conflict frames and the use of deception: Are competitive negotiators less ethical? *Journal of Applied Social Psychology, 35*, 2123-2149.

Schweitzer, M. E., Hershey, J. C., & Bradlow, E. T. (2006). Promises and lies: Restoring violated trust. *Organizational Behavior and Human Decision Processes, 101*, 1-19.

Semega, J., Kollar, M., Shrider, E. A., & Creamer, J. (2020). *Income and poverty in the United States: 2019*. U.S. Census Bureau, Current Population Reports, P60-270 (RV). Washington, D.C.: U.S. Government Publishing Office. https://www.census.gov/library/publications/2020/demo/p60-270.html

Shan, W., Keller, J., & Imai, L. (2016). What's a masculine negotiator? What's a feminine negotiator? It depends on the cultural and situational contexts. *Negotiation and Conflict Management Research, 9*(1), 22-43.

Shan, W., Keller, J., & Joseph, D. (2019). Are men better negotiators everywhere? A meta-analysis of how gender differences in negotiation performance vary across cultures. *Journal of Organizational Behavior, 40*(6), 651-675.

Shapiro, D. L., Sheppard, B. H., & Cheraskin, L. (1992). Business on a handshake. *Negotiation Journal, 8*(4), 365-377.

Sharma, S., Bottom, W. P., & Elfenbein, H. A. (2013). On the role of personality, cognitive ability, and emotional intelligence in predicting negotiation outcomes: A meta-analysis. *Organizational Psychology Review, 3*(4), 293-336.

Sheffield, J. (1995). The effect of communication medium on negotiation performance. *Group Decision and Negotiation, 4*(2), 159-179.

Sherif, M., Taub, D., & Hovland, C. I. (1958). Assimilation and contrast effects of anchoring stimuli on judgments. *Journal of Experimental Psychology, 55*(2), 150-155.

Siegel, S., & Fouraker, L. E. (1960). *Bargaining and group decision making: Experiments in bilateral monopoly*. New York: McGraw-Hill.

SimanTov-Nachlieli, I., Har-Vardi, L., & Moran, S. (2020). When negotiators with honest reputations are less (and more) likely to be deceived. *Organizational Behavior and Human Decision Processes, 157*, 68-84.

Sinaceur, M. (2010). Suspending judgment to create value: Suspicion and trust in negotiation. *Journal of Experimental Social Psychology, 46*(3), 543-550.

Sinaceur, M., Maddux, W., Vasiljevic, D., Nuckel, R., & Galinsky, A. (2013). Good things come to those who wait. *Personality and Social Psychology Bulletin, 39*(6), 814-825.

Small, D. A., Gelfand, M., Babcock, L., & Gettman, H. (2007). Who goes to the bargaining table? The influence of gender and framing on the initiation of negotiation. *Journal of Personality and Social Psychology, 93*(4), 600-613.

Smith, D. H. (1969). Communication and negotiation outcome. *Journal of Communication, 19*(3), 248-256.

Steinel, W., Utz, S., & Koning, L. (2010, November). The good, the bad and the ugly thing to do when sharing information: Revealing, concealing and lying depend on social motivation, distribution and importance of information. *Organizational Behavior and Human Decision Processes, 113*(2), 85-96.

Stevens, C. K., & Gist, M. E. (1997). Effects of self-efficacy and goal-orientation training on negotiation skill maintenance: What are the mechanisms? *Personnel Psychology, 50*(4), 955-978.

Stevens, C. K., Bavetta, A. G., & Gist, M. E. (1993). Gender differences in the acquisition of salary negotiation skills: The role of goals, self-efficacy, and perceived control. *Journal of Applied Psychology, 78*(5), 723-735.

Stillinger, C. A. (1988). *The reactive devaluation barrier to conflict resolution (Vol. 3).* Stanford, CA: Stanford Center on Conflict and Negotiation, Stanford University.

Strudler, A. (1995). On the ethics of deception in negotiation. *Business Ethics Quarterly, 5*(4), 805-822.

Stuhlmacher, A. F., & Citera, M. (2005). Hostile behavior and profit in virtual negotiation: A meta-analysis. *Journal of Business and Psychology, 20*(1), 69-93.

Stuhlmacher, A. F., & Linnabery, E. (2013). Gender and negotiation: A social role analysis. In M. Olekalns, & W. Adair (Eds.), *Handbook of research on negotiation* (pp. 221-248). Cheltenham, UK and Northampton, MA, USA: Edward Elgar Publishing.

Stuhlmacher, A. F., & Walters, A. E. (1999). Gender differences in negotiation outcome: A meta-analysis. *Personnel Psychology, 52*(3), 653-677.

Stuhlmacher, A. F., Citera, M., & Willis, T. (2007). Gender differences in virtual negotiation: Theory and research. *Sex Roles, 57*(5), 329-339.

Swaab, R. I., Galinsky, A. D., Medvec, V., & Diermeier, D. A. (2012). The communication orientation model: Explaining the diverse effects of sight, sound, and synchronicity on negotiation on group decision-making outcomes. *Personality and Social Psychology Review, 16*(1), 25-53.

Sycara, K., Gelfand, M., & Abbe, A. (Eds.) (2013). *Models for intercultural collaboration and negotiation.* New York: Springer.

Tenbrunsel, A. E. (1998). Misrepresentation and expectations of misrepresentation in an ethical dilemma: The role of incentives and temptation. *Academy of Management Journal, 41*(3), 330-339.

Tenbrunsel, A. E., & Messick, D. M. (1999). Sanctioning systems, decision frames, and cooperation. *Administrative Science Quarterly, 44*(4), 684-707.

Tenbrunsel, A. E., & Messick, D. M. (2001). Power asymmetries and the ethical atmosphere in negotiations. In J. M. Darley, D. M. Messick, & T. R. Tyler (Eds.), *Social influences on ethical behavior in organizations* (pp. 201-216). Mahwah, NJ: Lawrence Erlbaum Associates Publishers.

Tey, K. S., Schaerer, M., Madan, N., & Swaab, R. I. (2021, July). The impact of concession patterns on negotiations: When and why decreasing concessions lead to a distributive disadvantage. *Organizational Behavior and Human Decision Processes, 165,* 153-166.

Thaler, R. (1992). *The winner's curse: Paradoxes and anomalies of economic life.* New York: Free Press.

Thibaut, J. W., & Kelley, H. H. (1959). *The social psychology of groups*. New York: Wiley.

Thompson, L. (1990). Negotiation behavior and outcomes: Empirical evidence and theoretical issues. *Psychological Bulletin, 108*(3), 515-532.

Thompson, L. (1995, November). The impact of minimum goals and aspirations on judgments of success in negotiations. *Group Decision and Negotiation, 4*, 513-524.

Thompson, L., & Hastie, R. (1990). Social perception in negotiation. *Organizational Behavior and Human Decision Processes, 47*, 98-123.

Thompson, L. L., & Hrebec, D. (1996). Lose–lose agreements in interdependent decision making. *Psychological Bulletin, 120*(3), 396-409.

Thompson, L., & Leonardelli, G. J. (2004, August). The big bang: The evolution of negotiation research. *Academy of Management Perspectives, 18*(3), 113-117.

Thompson, L. L., & Nadler, J. (2002). Negotiating via information technology: Theory and application. *Journal of Social Issues, 58*(1), 109-124.

Thompson, L. L., Valley, K. L., & Kramer, R. M. (1995, November). The bitter-sweet feeling of success: An examination of social perception in negotiation. *Journal of Experimental Social Psychology, 31*(6), 467-492.

Tinsley, C. H., & Brett, J. M. (2001, July). Managing workplace conflict in the United States and Hong Kong. *Organizational Behavior and Human Decision Processes, 85*(2), 360-381.

Tinsley, C. H., O'Connor, K. M., & Sullivan, B. A. (2002). Tough guys finish last: The perils of a distributive reputation. *Organizational Behavior and Human Decision Processes, 88*(2), 621-642.

Tng, H.-Y., & Au, A. C. (2014). Strategic display of anger and happiness in negotiation: The moderating role of perceived authenticity. *Negotiation Journal, 30*(3), 301-327.

Toosi, N. R., Semnani-Azad, Z., Shen, W., Mor, S., & Amanatullah, E. T. (2020). How culture and race shape gender dynamics in negotiation. In M. Olekalns, & J. A. Kennedy (Eds.), *Research handbook on gender and negotiation* (pp. 260-280). Cheltenham, UK and Northampton, MA, USA: Edward Elgar Publishing.

Trevino, L. K., den Nieuwenboer, N. A., & Kish-Gephart, J. J. (2014). (Un) ethical behavior in organizations. *Annual Review of Psychology, 65*, 635-660.

Triandis, H. C. (2018). *Individualism and collectivism*. London: Routledge.

Trotschel, R., Bundgrens, S., Huffmeier, J., & Loschelder, D. D. (2013). Promoting prevention success at the bargaining table: Regulatory focus in distributive negotiation. *Journal of Economic Psychology, 38*, 26-39.

Trotschel, R., Loschelder, D. D., Hohne, B. P., & Majer, J. M. (2015). Procedural frames in negotiations: How offering my resources versus requesting yours impact perception, behavior, and outcomes. *Journal of Personality and Social Psychology, 108*(35), 417-435.

Trotschel, R., Huffmeier, J., Loschelder, D. D., Schwartz, K., & Gollwitzer, P. M. (2011). Perspective taking as a means to overcome motivational barriers in negotiations: When putting oneself into the opponent's shoes helps to walk toward agreements. *Journal of Personality and Social Psychology, 101*(4), 771-790.

Turnbull, A. A., Strickland, L., & Shaver, K. G. (1976). Medium of communication, differential power, and phasing of concessions: Negotiating success and attributions to the opponent. *Human Communication Research, 2*(3), 262-270.

Tversky, A., & Kahneman, D. (1974, September). *Judgment under uncertainty: Heuristics and biases. Science, 185*(4157), 1124-1131.

Tversky, A., & Kahneman, D. (1981, January 30). The framing of decisions and and the psychology of choice. *Science, 211*(4481), 453-458. Retrieved from https://www.jstor.org/stable/1685855

Tyler, T. R., Rasinski, K. A., & Spodick, N. (1985). Influence of voice on satisfaction with leaders: Exploring the meaning of process control. *Journal of Personality and Social Psychology, 48*(1), 72-81.

Valley, K. L., Moag, J., & Bazerman, M. H. (1998). "A matter of trust": Effects of communication on the efficiency and distribution of outcomes. *Journal of Economic Behavior and Organization, 34*(2), 211-238.

Valley, K. L., Neale, M. A., & Mannix, E. A. (1995). Friends, lovers, colleagues, stranger: The effects of relationships on the process and outcomes of dyadic negotiations. In B. H. Sheppard, R. J. Lewicki, & R. H. Bies (Eds.), *Research on negotiation in organizations* (Vol. 5, pp. 65-93). Mahwah, NJ: Lawrence Erlbaum Associates Publishers.

van Kleef, G. A., & Van Lange, P. M. (2008). What other's disappointment may do to selfish people: Emotion and social value orientation in a negotiation context. *Personality and Social Psychology Bulletin, 34*(8), 1084-1095.

van Kleef, G. A., Anastasopoulou, C., & Nijstad, B. A. (2010, November). Can expression of anger enhance creativity? A test of the emotions as social information (EASI) model. *Journal of Experimental Social Psychology, 46*(6), 1042-1048.

van Kleef, G. A., DeDreu, C. K., & Manstead, A. R. (2006). Supplication and appeasement in conflict and negotiation. The interpersonal effects of disappointment, worry, guilt and regret. *Journal of Personality and Social Psychology, 91*(1), 124-142.

Van Lange, P. A., De Bruin, E., Otten, W., & Joireman, J. A. (1997). Development of prosocial, individualistic, and competitive orientations: Theory and preliminary evidence. *Journal of Personality and Social Psychology, 73*(4), 733-746.

Volkema, R., Kapoutsis, I., & Nikolopoulos, A. (2013). Initiation behavior in negotiations: The moderating role of motivation on the ability–intentionality relationship. *Negotiation and Conflict Management Research, 6*(1), 32-48.

von Neumann, J., & Morgenstern, O. (1944). *Theory of games and economic behavior.* Princeton, NJ: Princeton University Press.

Walters, A. E., Stuhlmacher, A. F., & Meyer, L. L. (1998). Gender and negotiator competitiveness: A meta-analysis. *Organizational Behavior and Human Decision Processes, 76*(1), 1-29.

Walther, J. B. (1992). Interpersonal effects in computer-mediated interaction: A relational perspective. *Communication Research, 19*(1), 52-90.

Walther, J. B. (1994). Anticipated ongoing interaction versus channel effects on relational communication in computer-mediated interaction. *Human Communication Research, 20*(4), 473-501.

Walton, R. E., & McKersie, R. B. (1965). *A behavioral theory of labor negotiations; an analysis of a social interaction system.* New York: McGraw-Hill.

Walton, R. E., Cutcher-Gershenfeld, J. E., & McKersie, R. B. (1994). *Strategic negotiations: A theory of change in labor–management relations.* Boston, MA: Harvard Business School Press.

Wang, C. S., & Leung, A. K. (2010). The cultural dynamics of rewarding honesty and punishing deception. *Personality and Social Psychology Bulletin, 36*(11), 1529-1542.

Wang, C. S., Leung, A. K., See, Y. H., & Gao, X. Y. (2011). The effects of culture and friendship on rewarding honesty and punishing deception. *Journal of Experimental Social Psychology, 47*(6), 1295-1299.

Wang, C. S., Whitson, J. A., Anicich, E. M., Kray, L. J., & Galinsky, A. D. (2017). Challenge your stigma: How to reframe and revalue negative stereotypes and slurs. *Current Directions in Psychological Science, 26*(1), 75-80.

Watson, D., Clark, L., & Tellegen, A. (1988, June). Development and validation of brief measures of positive and negative affect: The PANAS scales. *Journal of Personality and Social Psychology, 54*(6), 1063-1070.

White, J. B., Tynan, R., Galinsky, A. D., & Thompson, L. L. (2004). Face threat sensitivity in negotiation: Roadblock to agreement and joint gain. *Organizational Behavior and Human Decision Processes, 94*(2), 102-124.

Wilson, K. S., DeRue, D. S., Matta, F. K., Howe, M., & Conlon, D. E. (2016). Personality similarity in negotiations: Testing the dyadic effects of similarity in interpersonal traits and the use of emotional displays on negotiation outcomes. *Journal of Applied Psychology, 101*(10), 1405-1421.

Wilson, T. D., Houston, C. E., Etling, K. M., & Brekke, N. (1996). A new look at anchoring effects: Basic anchoring and its antecedents. *Journal of Experimental Psychology: General, 125*(4), 387-402.

Wong, E. M., Haselhaun, M. P., & Kray, L. J. (2012). Improving the future by considering the past. The impact of upward counterfactual reflection and implicit beliefs on negotiation performance. *Journal of Experimental Social Psychology, 48*(1), 403-406.

Yamagishi, T., Cook, K. S., & Watabe, M. (1998). Uncertainty, trust, and commitment formation in the United States and Japan. *American Journal of Sociology, 104*(1), 165-194.

Yuan, Y., Head, M., & Du, M. (2003). The effects of multimedia communication on the web-based negotiation. *Group Decision and Negotiation, 12*(2), 89-109.

Yukl, G. A. (1974). Effects of the opponent's initial offer, concession magnitude and concession frequency on bargaining behavior. *Journal of Personality and Social Psychology, 30*(3), 323-335.

Zajonc, R. B. (1968). Cognitive theories in social psychology. In G. Lindzey & E. Aronson (Eds.), *Handbook of social psychology* (2nd ed., Vol. 1, pp. 320-411). Reading, MA: Addison-Wesley.

Zajonc, R. B. (1980). Feeling and thinking: Preferences need no inferences. *American Psychologist, 35*(2), 151-175.

Zechmeister, K., & Druckman, D. (1973). Determinants of resolving a conflict of interest: A simulation of political decision-making. *Journal of Conflict Resolution, 17*(1), 63-88.

Zerres, A., Huffmeier, J., Freund, P. A., Backhaus, K., & Hertel, G. (2013). Does it take two to tango? Longitudinal effects of unilateral and bilateral integrative negotiation training. *Journal of Applied Psychology, 98*(3), 478-491.

Index

Titles in the **Elgar Advanced Introductions** series include: